D0410620

OUT OF THE EVIL NIGHT

OUT OF THE EVIL NIGHT

LEIF HOVELSEN

Translated from the Norwegian
by John Morrison

BLANDFORD PRESS · LONDON

PUBLISHED 1959

16 West Central Street, London, W.C.1
Second Edition (revised) 1960

First published in Norway (Oslo 1958)
under the title "All Verden Venter"
Second Norwegian Edition, April 1959

Printed in Great Britain by Richard Clay and Company, Ltd.,
Bungay, Suffolk

CONTENTS

PREFACE

THIS book scarcely fits into any of the usual literary categories. It records facts and events just as I experienced them. Deliberately, I have used only material of which I had first-hand knowledge and the people whom the book describes in detail have themselves approved of what is set down about them. Names from the war period have, for the most part, been omitted.

I am particularly glad that 'Out of the Evil Night' has been translated into English. During the war years we learned to listen eagerly for the 'V' signal, the repeated dot-dot-dot-dash on the air that always came before the words—'Here is London', and then the news. We listened for that dot-dot-dot-dash, the familiar opening rhythm of Beethoven's Fifth, often in the most extraordinary places and situations. We felt one with the British people, felt a common destiny with them, and so the ties between our two countries are very strong.

In writing this book it is my conviction that we still need one another. I have wanted to pass on these experiences and ideas about the times through which we are living because the struggle going on in the world today is just as crucial, if not more so, as the actual warfare of the 1940's.

So I am more than grateful that 'Out of the Evil Night' is now being made available to the English-speaking people, on whom so much depends and for whom I feel such a warm friendship. I would like to record my gratitude to my friend John Morrison, who made the translation from the Norwegian and has given constant and invaluable help in preparing this English edition, and especially for his contribution towards the chapter "Road to Europe".

LEIF HOVELSEN

Oslo, May 1959

I

The Evil Night

THERE was a knock on the door. The nurse who had been living with us during the war stuck her head in. 'There's someone outside asking for you,' she said.

From the window I could see a figure in the dusk standing motionless and half hidden by the lilac bushes right underneath.

'Come down,' said a low voice, 'I have information for you from Hans.' Hans was one of my contacts in the Resistance.

'Who are you?' I called back. No answer. I asked again.

'Come down,' repeated the voice.

'Unless you tell me who you are I'll ring up the police,' I called back. Then I shut the window, got into bed and pulled the quilt up over me.

I was afraid. Something must have gone wrong. Suddenly there was a sound of breaking glass and heavy footsteps on the stairs. The door was flung open. The Gestapo! They pulled me out of bed and handcuffed me. Mother and father looked on with shocked faces.

'What has he done?' mother asked.

'Plenty,' was the answer and they took me into the other room. While two of them questioned me, three others ransacked the house. They found nothing. By good luck they did not look under the floor in the passage, where four radio receivers were stowed away. I said to them that they must have come to the wrong house and that there must have been some mix-up. However, they showed me a piece of paper.

'This is your name and address. We're going to take you down to headquarters. There we'll get you to talk all right.'

I got dressed and they took me out to the car. As they pushed me in I heard mother's voice from the verandah. Her voice shook as she called, 'Leif, don't forget Jesus.'

I could feel myself getting red. 'Jesus,' I thought, 'that's only for old women and invalids.' It was embarrassing.

In the twenty minutes it took to drive to Victoria Terrace (the Gestapo headquarters in Oslo) my brain was working feverishly. That piece of paper with my name and address? Information from Hans, they had said. Could it be . . . ?

In the streets everything was still. Not a person in sight. Not even a light anywhere. Only ourselves in the grey dark of a summer night—the 9th of June 1943. I was nineteen and had just finished my school finals.

They continued questioning me in the car. I played innocent, as if I knew nothing, but deep down inside I was anxious. I knew too much.

At Victoria Terrace I was taken into a big room. Norwegian and German Gestapo men were shouting to one another. Four of them bombarded me with most searching questions and stuck a bundle of illegal news sheets under my nose. However, luck was with me. After a few hours I was taken in the Black Maria to Møller Street 19 (the central Oslo jail). I relaxed and felt rather proud that I had hoodwinked the Gestapo.

I was put into Cell B24.

2

The Dawning

I

THE door clanged shut. I was alone, locked in. I threw my full weight against the door. No use. It was too strong. I looked around. The window? It was securely barred. There was no way out.

In the cell there was a bed and an old school desk on which was lying a spoon. On the floor there was a wash-basin and a mug of water. In one corner near the door there was a little shutter in the wall. This I opened curiously. It stank.

I thought of the questioning I had been through and of the answers I had given. They had only asked me about illegal newspapers. I began to feel a bit more confident. They could not possibly know about the other things I had been in on. I felt sure I would be out again for Christmas.

With a clang a grill in the door was opened. Meal-time. Stinking fish and rotten potatoes. No, thank you. I let it stand untouched. Only later did it dawn on me that this was the main meal of the day. Mornings and evenings it was ersatz coffee with a few slices of bread and a little margarine and, now and then, a bit of goat's cheese. I soon got so hungry that I took whatever they brought.

The first days seemed like weeks. On the back of the wooden window shutters I discovered a series of small marks arranged in groups of seven. They must have served as a calendar. One prisoner had been here forty days, another fifty. The one with the longest row had been here ninety days. But after I had made the fifth mark with my nail I exclaimed: 'How on earth can I hold out in here?'

One day I began to reckon. If I stayed in the cell a year that would make 365 marks. But if I were to live another fifty years in freedom that would make 18,250 days. A mere 365 was nothing to worry about, and one day was nothing compared with the time I would spend in freedom. Every day would bring me a step nearer the goal. This simple calculation gave me fresh courage. As the days passed and nothing happened I became more and more sure that everything would be all right.

My friend Per, who had been in the same class at school with me, must certainly have got safely to Sweden by now and I could feel safe. Together we had been distributing short-wave radio receivers in different parts of the country. We had even come to school with them in our rucksacks. The past two years had certainly been full of adventure. Now I had landed here. But one thing I promised myself—I would never incriminate any of my friends, cost what it might.

To make the time pass I took to whistling. It might be 'Ave Maria', Handel's 'Largo', a folk tune, or a march. One afternoon when I was having a music session something happened. It must have been when I was lustily whistling 'Løft ditt hode, du raske gutt' ('Up with your head, you lively boy') by the window. Suddenly I could hear the same tune coming back. Was it an echo? No, it must be someone answering. I whistled another tune. That too was repeated. I must try to find out a little more. I whistled the student song 'Gaudeamus igitur'. Just as quickly it was answered. Was the unknown a student? Next I tried a few special songs of our final student year. Whoever was replying knew them all, even some we had sung at one certain party. I was beginning to get a little anxious. Could it be Per? After a minute's thought I tried one or two hymns I could remember from home. Per was the son of a missionary and we had both been in the high school's Christian student group. Each hymn was answered. Was it then . . .? No, it couldn't be, it mustn't be Per. Then I tried our own class song. If he answered this one it could only be Per. There was no answer. I whistled it again. Everything was quiet. I danced for joy in my cell. I could be sure still that he had got away and was safe in Sweden.

Equally surprising and enjoyable as the musical contest was a package of clothes from my mother which the guard brought in unexpectedly one day. As I took the clothes in my hands, I found that each article she had sent had my initials neatly embroidered on it in light green, the colour of hope. It was so like her. There was no doubt about what she had in mind. I could just picture her sitting there on the verandah getting the clothes ready.

I thought about my mother. Something had come between us lately. I no longer had the faith she had. From my boyhood we had always gone to church together. But in my last year in high school I had acquired a voracious appetite for everything I thought was 'radical' and 'revolutionary', and I reacted more and more against our Christian background. It was so narrow. I drank in Garborg and Bjørnson. How much I understood of them I don't know, but I was gripped by their violent attack on conventional Christianity and enthusiastic over their break with tradition. To be honest, I felt the same myself. I could no longer bear to be 'right-thinking'. One spring day as I was coming out of school I said to myself, 'I want to be free and I want to be radical.' I didn't say a word to mother or father about it—nor to anyone else. But at home they certainly had a feeling of what was brewing.

At last I could keep it to myself no longer. Mother wept. It was not that I wanted to hurt her. I only wanted to be honest. She herself was not at all narrow. On the contrary she had a lively interest in whatever was happening in our own country, and in the rest of the world too. She was always the last to put out the light at night, for she was always sitting reading. Yet faith meant everything to her.

By this time I had begun to read psychology and philosophy. One day I discovered Karl Marx. I found a copy of 'The

Communist Manifesto' on one of my uncle's bookshelves, took it home with me, and read it in secret. But none of this gave me what I was looking for. I kept on searching.

What occupied me more than anything else was the fight for our freedom. That was reality and no one could avoid taking responsibility. As well as listening to the daily news from London and passing it on, and distributing our illegal newspapers, I delivered small short-wave receivers to various contacts. I had one of my own at home, which I had secretly installed under the writing desk.

One afternoon after I had hurried into my room to 'do my lessons' (I was going to listen in to the 3 p.m. news) mother got a bit suspicious of my striking interest in my school work. Unexpectedly she came into the room while I was under the table listening in. I had forgotten to lock the door. I thought it would be the end of listening-in, at home anyway. With a twinkle in her eye she said, 'Could you get an extra pair of headphones?' After that we often sat together listening-in, and father joined us too.

Father was not unadventurous. His passion was skiing. Round the turn of the century times were difficult in the building trades (which was his work), so he went to America and got a job in Chicago, but all the time he longed for the ski slopes back home and wished he were back in the North.

In his time he won every skiing trophy possible. His best year was perhaps 1903 when he won the top prizes for both racing and jumping—the fifty kilometre race, the King's Cup and the Holmenkollen gold medal.

One summer day when he was taking a walk in a Chicago park, he saw a chute where small boats shot down into the water and then were pulled up again. At once he thought that it would be possible to slide down it on skis. He talked to the people running the show and got permission to try. He smeared the bottom of the skis with soap, took off from the top and landed several yards out in the water. By this time he was travelling so fast that he skimmed along the top of the water on his skis for quite a bit before he began to sink. Then he kicked off the skis and swam ashore.

He was amusing himself doing this one day when the director of the famous Barnum and Bailey Circus saw him. He was so interested that he asked father if he could do something similar indoors, in the circus. The upshot was that he was engaged and from then on became 'The Flying Norseman'—the greatest sensation in Barnum and Bailey's 'Greatest Show on Earth'. He appeared in Madison Square Garden and all over America wherever the circus went. The newspapers reported that 'strong men turned away their faces and went white as their shirts and lovely ladies fainted with fear' when they saw him jump. There was a take-off built up over thirty yards and between the take-off point and the landing runway there was a gap of over fifteen yards. Sometimes two elephants would be stationed in the gap and he would make the jump over them. Four million people saw him jump.

He went later to Colorado and became a farmer. He also taught Americans skiing there and was known as 'The Father of Skiing in Colorado'. The biggest ski jump there bears his name, Hovelsen Hill.

In 1922 he took a trip to Norway to the celebration of his parents' golden wedding. That was when he met my mother. They were married and bought the wooden house which is still our home. It lies in Høybraten in the east end of Oslo.

Father was always a daredevil. He was only twelve when he was one of the few youngsters who tried the Huseby jump, used for national competitions until the days of the famous Holmenkollen jump. He slipped in and tried it after the competition was over. He is reckoned to be the oldest man to win a prize in the Holmenkollen jumping. At fifty years of age he was fifth in the oldest class. Mother has told me that I was only two when he first got me on to skis. He started racing down the steep slope just outside the house, with me between his knees, while mother stood looking out of the kitchen window with her heart in her mouth—but rather proud all the same.

I have many memories of father, and there alone in the cell they all began coming back to me—memories of summer holidays spent trout fishing in the streams and lakes, of winter time and wonderful ski trips. It all came back to me, and reliving it made the long hours pass quickly.

II

One evening I heard the sound of iron-shod boots in the corridor. The key grated in the lock and the door flew open.

'Four thousand seven hundred and eighty-five,' I said, as required. 'Get out!' shouted the guard. Out in the corridor were three Gestapo officers. They stood me up facing the wall. I waited tensely. Suddenly handcuffs were snapped on my left wrist and I was pulled roughly round. There in front of me stood Per! I felt like sinking through the stone paving. All I had been building my hopes on collapsed like a pack of cards. I felt despair. How much did they know? They handcuffed us together and drove us to Victoria Terrace. There we were separated. They took Per into another room and we were not to meet again till after the liberation and he came home from the Sachsenhausen concentration camp outside Berlin.

The next shock I got was when I was taken up before six of the Gestapo for further questioning. The first questions made it very clear that they had excellent information about us and knew things they could only have found out from our own people. Knowing too that Per was not in Sweden made me feel so at a loss that I had no clue what to do.

That night I shall never forget. At one point two of them twisted my arms back while a third hit me in the face with his clenched fist. I was powerless against them and finally gave the names of three of my friends. They also got me to make a sketch of the secret hiding-place at home where we had stowed the radios. Suddenly they got the idea that they would take me home with them.

'Perhaps the radios may have gone,' they said. 'Maybe your father has made off with them.'

'He doesn't know anything about them,' I replied, 'and I don't want to go home. You can find the radios yourselves. They are there under the passage way.'

'So you don't want to come home with us,' they laughed mockingly. One of them poked a revolver into my back. 'Get along or you'll get shot. We're not worried by corpses.' Again I was handcuffed and prodded into the car.

Fortunately the radios were there where I had said.

Next morning in the grey dawn I was taken back to Møller Street 19. I was at my wits' end with despair, felt myself doubly a failure, and so humiliated that it hurt. I begged the guard for a bed. The request was scornfully rejected. I gave up and lay down on the floor. Pictures of all that had happened that night kept coming to my mind over and over.

The thing that was like a knife in my heart was that I had given the three names. In spite of having promised myself, in spite of efforts to hold out, the Gestapo had been able to break me—I who had wanted to be the strong man and to show that I could be!

Then there was the scene outside Victoria Terrace as the Germans were pushing me into the car. A stranger came up to them, a Norwegian who had been standing there waiting. He was smelling of spirits, untidy and unshaven, as with shifty eyes he stretched out greedy hands saying 'When do I get the money?'

Then there was a third stab—the realisation that it might after all have been Hans, my comrade Hans, who had informed on us. It could have been from him they had got that piece of paper the night the Gestapo arrested me. They had been right, the others at home. 'You are too trusting, Leif,' they had said. 'Be careful with Hans.' I wouldn't listen to them and was annoyed that they could not understand that men were good. 'Edel sei der Mensch, hilfreich und gut.' Now all that I had built upon and trusted in had fallen to pieces, undermined and overwhelmed by the wave of evil that I had refused to take as reality.

Worst of all was the fear of what might happen next. The questioning had gone on for ten hours. At one point I had had the chance of glancing over what they had lying on the table—photographs of two friends of mine I thought were free. Presumably they too had been betrayed and arrested at the same time as myself.

It made my spine shiver when I thought of the two of them. What would happen if the things forced out of them did not correspond with what I had said? The thought would not leave me. I was clear on one point. So far I had been able to keep back the most important bit of information, but if they were going to question me again and use torture I would not be able to hold out. Then they might be able to get out of me who was responsible for the escape route to Sweden and who was the contact man with the Home Front. That would be catastrophe. What was I to do? Could I get word to these friends of mine? Probably they too were in Møller Street 19. I looked round the cell. It was hopeless. The guards? There was no one I could trust.

Like a flash of lightning the thought came—'Why not pray?' 'Pray! I don't believe in prayer.' 'Couldn't you try anyway?' 'But there's no sense in that.' 'It still might help. In any case it wouldn't hurt to try.' I had never been in such need. I was completely helpless.

I argued with myself to and fro for a while and then decided to make the experiment. 'God, if You exist,' I prayed, 'and You are here and see everything, then You know how helpless I am and what is at stake.' And I prayed: 'Will You help Odd and Fridtjof to get through and say the right things. And God,' I added, 'if You can give me an answer and proof that You exist then I will give myself fully and wholly to You. I want to believe but how can I believe if I don't know?'

A few days later, on a Monday afternoon, the door opened and the guard came in with the prison barber. That was strange, for I knew it was not my turn yet. I was taken down to Corridor A and placed on a stool right by the exit to the courtyard. The barber, who was a prisoner himself, began to cut my hair while the German guard looked on. The barber turned the stool a bit to the left, perhaps it was accidentally, but at the same moment steps were heard on the stairs up above and four men came marching down. It was my two friends, Odd and Fridtjof, followed by two guards! They halted in the corridor only a few yards away and saw me at once. The Germans began talking with one another and like lightning Odd leaned towards me and told about the questioning he had been through. With one eye on the guards I whispered back, 'That's exactly what I said too.'

We had to wait several more minutes and then another chance came and I whispered to Fridtjof, 'I don't know you but I know your brother.'

'That's what I told them,' he shot back. 'We're being taken to Grini.' [1]

Soon after they were taken out through the iron doors to the courtyard, where a car was waiting. One last encouraging smile and they were gone.

When I got back to B24 I was exulting. 'That is terrific,' I thought and did a dance for joy. Suddenly I remembered my prayer.

'But,' I argued, 'it could be just chance.' 'Chance yourself!' 'Well it was a very natural thing for the barber to turn me to the left. He does it to everybody. It wasn't so very strange that my two friends were taken out either. Things like that do happen.' I paused. 'But what about the remarkable way we were able to talk to one another and exchange these important sentences right under the eyes of the guards?' 'Just chance?' 'Well, but then why was it that I out of 450 prisoners should have been given a

[1] Grini—the dreaded Nazi concentration camp north-west of Oslo.

haircut on that particular day and at the very time they were being taken to Grini?'

There was thunder outside and it grew dark in the cell. I felt very small and humble. I burst out, 'God, I believe.' I wept. From that moment I had something new, an inner conviction that I felt could never be shaken.

However much reasoning might try to prove the whole thing was a coincidence, I knew deep in my heart that God had given a miracle, not only in outward circumstances but inside me. I was different. Peace, confidence, joy and patience had come and were sustaining me. It no longer seemed the most important thing whether I remained a week or a year in solitary confinement. Life suddenly seemed to me the most wonderful gift.

Every day I discovered new values. It might be a verse from Ibsen's 'Brand', which I had learned at school, whose meaning I suddenly realised:

> 'Sjel, vær trofast til det siste.
> Seirens seir er alt å miste.
> Tapets alt din vinning skapte.
> Evig eies kun det tapte!' [1]

Now I began to understand what freedom really was, what we had to fight for, and what a gift it was to have been able to go to school, to read and learn, to have parents and a good home. Now for the first time when everything had been taken from me it all came alive for me. In an instant B24 had become an entirely different world. Life had meaning.

Of course there were difficult times, and there were days when I was taken for further intensive questioning by the Gestapo. But now I was the one who was on the offensive. A new source of power opened when I prayed and constantly told God of the difficulties I was up against.

[1] Soul, be steadfast to the end.
The victor's victory is to lose all.
Lost is all that your effort has won,
Possessed for ever only the lost.

After I had been a further month in B24 I was questioned again, this time by a Norwegian Gestapo agent. He was drunk. The first thing he wanted to know was the name and address of a school comrade. He had obviously got hold of some information and he made it clear I was the only one who could give the name and address. I had no idea how I could get out of it. I knew what he was after. But whatever the cost I was determined he would not get it from me. So I protested ignorance till at last he gave up. Then he tried to get information from me about a Communist group which supplied our secret printing press with news. 'We know you know them,' he said. 'This is your chance. Tell us and we'll no longer class you a Communist.'

'I am no Communist,' I replied.

'The devil you're not!' he answered. 'You're mixed up with Communism but if you tell what you know about them we can promise you won't be shot. If you won't tell, it's all up with you.'

The alternatives were clear. If I told what I knew it would bring the Communist group into danger. If I kept silent it could cost me my life. It was as if some power came from above. I decided not to give him any information and continued to pretend ignorance. It worked. I was sent back to my cell without having given anything away.

Only now did I begin to realise that I was in worse danger than I had thought. Two weeks previously the Gestapo official dealing with my case had hinted that I would be executed, but at that time I didn't really believe it. Now the truth dawned—Execution! For what? Everything in me shouted to be let live. I could not grasp that this might be the end. Especially now when I had just begun to discover the real secret of living.

I knew that prayer was my one hope through the experience I had had two months previously. 'Whatever be Your will, God,' I said, 'let that come to pass. But if I may live and even be free once again, I give You the whole of my life for You to use as You will.'

In the days that followed I began to think about Christ. Up to then I felt I did not understand Him. But now, having been betrayed and beaten and standing face to face with death, all He had gone through became real to me. What He had suffered was far far more than what was happening to me. It was like Jesus walking by my side and saying to me, 'Don't be afraid. I have done all this for you. I am conqueror.'

These were the richest days I have ever lived through.

Often I thought back to my boyhood days, when I went to church with my mother. I went gladly, to accompany her. I didn't listen much to the sermon, it is true, but I liked the organ music and the singing. What impressed me most was the communion service, though I did not understand a great deal of it. The service was sung in our church and I could clearly hear the voice of the priest: 'In the same night that He was betrayed, He took bread and, when He had given thanks, He brake it . . .' Now I sang the words and more than anything else they supported me through these days. It brought joy and patience and an inner peace whatever might happen. In the evenings a feeling of loneliness might come over me. Then I would sing, 'Lead kindly light amid the encircling gloom, Lead thou me on.' I was in fellowship with God. What more did I need?

Every time I heard the sound of jack-boots and the key turning in the lock the thought would go through me, 'Is it my turn this time?' One morning as I was pacing B24 and heard the steps of the guard in the corridor, the thought struck me, 'That German is an unhappy man. Perhaps he feels just like a slave and has to do all this against his will. He is condemned to be part of an evil system and can't find any way out.' Or again, 'Germany will lose the war, not because of us Allies, but because she has turned against God and is using these evil means to reach her goal. That way lies no progress. However long it may take the result is certain.' Brand's words, 'The victor's victory is to lose all. Lost is all that your effort has won, Possessed for ever only the lost,' now took on a new meaning in a much wider perspective. 'When the time comes that Germany is defeated and her pride broken there will be the possibility of her finding God and advancing to a new life as a nation.'

The days came and went. One morning as I was pacing to and fro in my cell I began quoting Shakespeare, 'To be or not to be that is the question.' I came to a halt and burst out laughing. That was really funny.

Another month went by. I was still alive.

III

I had just eaten the midday meal when the guard came and summoned me. Down the corridor I observed one of the higher Gestapo officers who had been present at several of the interrogations but in the background. He asked me to sit opposite him at the table. I took a good look at him. He was a tall, slim, blond German, certainly one of those considered 'pure Aryan'. On the surface he seemed quite attractive, with sharp, clear features, but there was something cold and calculating in his look.

I took the initiative. 'I have been four months in solitary confinement now,' I said, 'without being allowed anything to read, or to write or get out in the fresh air. I would like permission to read. I'm just wasting time. I should have been at the university by now.'

He laughed. 'Wasting your time? That's your own fault. Why did you join the Resistance Movement?'

He talked on for half an hour or more. He spoke about the Nazi ideology and put the case for it in a very persuasive manner. He described what Hitler had done for Germany and gave an enthusiastic account of the victorious advance of the German armies across the whole of Europe. The war would soon be over. 'We're advancing in Italy,' he said. That was the first I had heard of fighting in Italy, so I concluded that the Allies had made a landing there. 'When we Germans have defeated the Allies,' he said, 'we will unite the continent and build the United States of Europe, similar to the United States of America.'

From there he went on to describe life in the Hitler Youth. With fire and warmth he spoke of the passion that had filled hundreds of thousands of young people with enthusiasm to play their part in the battle for a new Europe. Every word and gesture showed me that he fully and firmly believed what he was saying. I felt it like a quicksand that I would have to fight against not to be dragged down.

Suddenly he asked, 'Do you want Russia and England to win the war?'

I thought for a moment. There sat the man who held my fate in his hands. I felt small and powerless before him. 'I don't want Russia and England or Germany to win the war,' I said. I knew I was on thin ice but what was I to do?

He changed the subject. 'If we set you free after two years and one of your friends came to you and asked, "Can you help us to print these illegal newspapers?" what would be your answer?'

'I have lost so much time sitting in prison that I must concentrate on my studies now,' I ventured.

'You expect me to believe that?' he asked.

I said nothing.

'You have been in solitary confinement quite a while,' he went on. 'If we put you in with some others so that you would have someone to talk to, how would you like that?'

'Very much.'

'Now suppose one of the others in the cell was taken for questioning. He comes back and tells how well he hoodwinked the Gestapo and that they got nothing out of him. Would you be willing to tell us that?'

I looked him in the eye and said, 'No.'

'Now look here,' he said, going on quickly. 'If you were freed to start at the university would you be willing to give us information on what goes on?'

'No.'

He smiled and continued, 'If we set you free now you could go ahead and finish your studies and get yourself a job, then would you be willing to give us information? We guarantee that no one would ever know about it.'

There was a pause. 'No,' I said and added, 'it would be against my conscience.'

He looked at me in astonishment. 'I don't understand you. You yourself were betrayed. It's a very natural thing.'

I could only say, 'I can't do it.'

Without replying he got up. As he reached the door he said, 'Think it over. I'll be back in a week.'

I never saw him again. Two days later I was removed from my cell and taken to Grini.

I often thought about that conversation later. It was coming face to face with something I had not understood up till then. Gradually I realised that I had come up against the force of an ideology, the challenge of men who were passionately committed to win and to use other men for their plan and collective will.

I learned later that Hans had met it too. He had been arrested shortly before me. The same questions had been put to him and he had let himself be taken in by the Gestapo's promises. As the price of freedom he had committed himself to telling all he knew about us. I was one of six who were arrested that night as a result.

He got out but not to freedom. On the contrary he got more and more entangled in the Gestapo's net. They never let him out of sight and squeezed him like a lemon for information. He was paid. He betrayed his own countrymen and took part in all sorts of interrogations at Victoria Terrace. Finally he lost all trace of humanity. The more he did, the less respect the Gestapo had for him and the less they trusted him. He was a pawn in their game—only as long as they needed him.

I trusted Hans. He was my friend. He chose himself the way he wanted to go, but I cannot bring myself to judge him. I had felt how small and helpless I was in face of those who would stop at nothing to break us down in order to use us. I knew that at the most critical moment it was not really I but my conscience which spoke the deciding 'No'. True I had tried to free myself from the faith of my parents and from Christian morality, but in misfortune and loneliness these values had come to life in me. They gave the clarity and strength I needed.

Well, I had stood up against Nazis, who wanted to get me in their power, but how to conquer an ideology like that, I had no idea. The question really was—faced with men who have given themselves completely to a false doctrine how is it possible to win them to something new?

It was when I got to Grini that I first met the man who taught me the way.

3
Cockcrow

THERE were twenty-five of us in the big green police bus as we were driven out of the city from Møller Street 19. It was a lovely autumn afternoon. I looked at everything with new eyes—every house, every tree, every passer-by—as we drove along. I hadn't expected to see it all again. Now it was all so near at hand and, at the same time, so far away. It was like being at the cinema, seeing wonderful, life-like pictures, yet they were not quite real.

About half an hour later we arrived at Grini. It is difficult to imagine what the name Grini conjures up to a Norwegian. It lies in a remote spot, in woodland country surrounded by hills that rise invitingly one above the other. Just before the war a prison for women had been built there. This had been converted into a concentration camp by the Germans, who had added twenty-five large barrack huts for living quarters and workshops. Outside the barbed-wire fence, sentry paths connected eight high watch-towers equipped with searchlights and machine guns. Beyond this there was a very high electrified fence and then a mine-field. Several thousand prisoners were kept interned there.

When we got to Grini I became Prisoner No. 8231 and was ordered to Hut 10 after going through the somewhat nerve-racking reception process and being issued the black prison garb and wooden shoes. I went into the hut. Its windows faced the electric fence and the woods beyond. It wasn't a big room but it was an advance on B24. There were bunks in tiers with room for twelve. I met my room-mates that evening. They welcomed me and were eager to hear how things were with me and what

I had been imprisoned for. It was the first time in four months that I had others to talk to. In the group were a business man, an architect, a few radical intellectuals, a fisherman, a sea captain —real, tough men all of them.

On the way to roll-call early next morning, whom should I run into but my friends Odd and Fridtjof, with whom I had been able to exchange those few whispered sentences in the Møller Street jail before their removal to Grini. We literally ran into one another's arms.

There is no need to give a detailed description of life in a concentration camp. That has been done often enough in the years since the war. I remained a prisoner at Grini for sixteen months and in these months three things especially etched themselves on my memory.

I

The same autumn that I was sent to Grini the Nazi police had carried out a raid on Oslo University and arrested many of the students and the professors. A large number of these were sent to Grini, among them a professor of history, a subject I had thought of studying. I determined to get to know him.

He was a slightly built man of medium height. I thought at first he seemed rather stern and unapproachable, but I soon discovered he had a warm heart and a fresh, boyish sense of humour. Actually he was Professor of Classics in the University, though he also lectured in history. He had been pointed out to me as a man of great integrity and I noticed that the way he thought and expressed himself had the logical clarity of the Latin scholar. We became friends.

Sunday was the only day of the week we were allowed to walk about freely inside the camp, and we used to take walks together along by the electric fence. In unforgettable conversations he gave life and shape to the fragments of history that I had learned at school. He made Socrates, Plato, Aristotle and the great figures of classical times live for me. And I noticed the professor was not only interested in my thinking but in what went on in my heart. He was interested in me as a person.

One day he began to tell me about himself. A few years before the war, he said, he had met a group of people who had given new direction to his life. He had been invited to a big meeting and, half hidden behind a pillar, had listened to the speakers and observed them carefully with objective reserve. They had spoken of absolute moral standards—absolute honesty, purity, unselfishness and love—as the measure each person could apply to his own life. They had spoken of change in men and in nations beginning with oneself. System after system had failed, and would continue to fail, unless the basic factor—human nature—was changed. As he listened he had felt how alone he was in spite of all his learning. These speakers had obviously found the thing he was longing for himself. He could see it in their faces. They radiated an inner freedom. Deep within himself he knew that what these people stood for was the biggest thing he had met in his life.

When he told me of the new life he had begun to live in their company, I asked him, 'What do you mean by what you called a quiet time? What is it?'

'To listen to God in order to receive His guidance,' he replied. 'What many of us have thought of as prayer is too often a monologue. It is like laying down the telephone receiver after you have said what you want to say.' It had been quite a new idea for him that perhaps God might have something to say too—that there might be places where one's life and work needed to be different.

'How do you go about this listening?' I asked.

'That is an experiment you must make for yourself,' he replied. 'Any time, anywhere you can stop and listen to that inner voice speaking. Write down the thoughts as they come.' He added with a twinkle in his eye, 'You may be surprised. If the thoughts you get agree with these four absolute standards you can be fairly sure they come from God.'

It sounded reasonable, though it took me some time before I ventured to try it myself. I found it hard to comprehend that God might be able to talk to me in that way.

One day light dawned. Early one winter morning I was standing by the electric fence looking out over the snowy landscape. Suddenly a thought hit me, 'You told a lie.' 'A lie?' 'Yes, you did not tell the whole truth to Steinar the other day.' Steinar had asked me if I had said anything about him when I was being questioned, and I had said no. The next thought was just as clear. 'What will you do?' Then it came with irresistible force, 'Go and tell the truth.' Was this what the professor meant by listening? 'No,' I thought, 'that's going too far. It's too ordinary.' But I could not get rid of the thought.

At that time Steinar was working in the book-bindery. I went to find him. But I turned back. Three times I tried and three times I could not bring myself to go in, though I knew that I could not get out of it.

One Sunday we went for half an hour's walk together and just before we parted I told him. Steinar held out his hand and as I took it he said, 'It's all right, Leif. I knew it.'

It drew us together as nothing else could. I was very glad.

II

It was in the spring, a day in May, that I got to know Olav. I think it was after a communion service that some of us had secretly attended in the disinfection hut. We came and went singly so as to avoid notice, and one of us always stood guard outside.

Olav was a few months older than I. He was a student, fairly tall, wore glasses, and characteristic of him were his clear thinking and his simple faith.

Many a time Olav and I strolled around the camp talking of the future, of our studies, and what we would do when we got home, sharing all our hopes and fears, joys and expectations, troubles and uncertainties.

One morning in early summer it all came to an end. Olav had told me earlier that he and four of his friends had been mixed up in the shooting of a Nazi policeman. This had been traced to them and the secret police were pressing the Germans for punishment. Olav and the other accused were taken to the court in Oslo and there condemned to death. In the afternoon they were back in one cell in the Grini prison. News of this spread among us at once.

Before the evening roll-call I walked under the window of the cell where the condemned men were. 'If only I could say something to encourage them. Olav, Thomas, Kai and Jan. If only I could . . .'

Many of the other prisoners were standing around waiting for roll-call. Among them were some of my comrades with whom I specially wanted to stand well, since I was eager to be just as 'radical' and 'intellectual' as they were. I nodded to them.

Then I saw Olav at the window. His hands were grasping the iron bars and he had pulled himself up so that he could see out. His eyes shone and his glance took us all in. Then he saw me and called in a strong, clear voice: 'Thanks for your comradeship, Leif. Never give up in the fight for Christ.'

I glanced at the others and kept quiet. I didn't answer. Depressed and ashamed I went back to the hut. I thought about Peter when he heard the cock crow.

The same night the condemned men were taken away. In the morning we heard that, before they were taken, Olav had read aloud:

'Who shall separate us from the love of Christ? Shall tribulation, or distress, or persecution, or famine, or nakedness, or peril, or sword?

'For I am persuaded, that neither death, nor life, nor angels, nor principalities, nor powers, nor things present, nor things to come, nor height, nor depth, nor any other creature, shall be able to separate us from the love of God, which is in Christ Jesus, our Lord.'

I missed Olav bitterly. But I decided never again to deny the truth of Christ that was given me in B24 and that I had seen in Olav's face that evening.

III

How were things going meantime with my own case? Most of us who were implicated in it were now in Grini and we kept together as much as we could. Rumour had it that it had been decided in Berlin to postpone the case and not let it come to trial for the time being. However, early in September some of us were suddenly taken to Victoria Terrace again. Some were questioned, others not. I was kept waiting for my turn, but evening came and we were taken back to Grini. The next day I was moved to 'Yellow Hut' together with two of the others. In this hut everyone wore a yellow triangle on the front and the back of the prison uniform, showing that a special set of restrictions applied to these prisoners.

The same morning Steinar and two others were put into the cell where Olav and his friends had spent their last day. I was afraid it might mean execution. In my need I sought out the professor and told him what had happened. We went out together and found a sheltered place behind Hut 10. It was one of these wonderful autumn days, clear and still. Beyond the electric fence a little red, wooden hut stood among the dark branches and everywhere the leaves were red and gold and brown. Here in the deep stillness we prayed together for Steinar and our friends.

A little later I caught a glimpse of him at the window. He seemed to be in good spirits, although he knew it might be his last day. 'I'll come back in the evening just before roll-call,' I called up to him. During the day I got a small piece of smoked meat, a bit of goat cheese and a few cigarettes. I wrote Steinar a letter and just before roll-call I was waiting below the window. A string came silently down and I quickly tied on the package. Next morning Steinar and the others were gone.

Some time after one of our mutual comrades told us what had happened. A Communist in our group had tried to smuggle out a letter containing a list of the Party members arrested at the same time as us. The letter was seized. Immediately after, those who were on the list, Steinar among them, were herded into a truck and driven off. We knew it was to execution. Not being a member of the Party, my name (and three others) was not listed.

At roll-call next day we four, who had all been implicated in the same case, were picked out along with thirty-six other prisoners. The word was that we were to be sent to Germany, to a liquidation camp, the rumour went. I wrote my parents a letter to keep up their courage, and got it smuggled out. With gallows' humour I put at the top of the letter: 'Norrønafolket, det vil fare, det vil føre kraft til andre.' [1]

Everything was set for our departure. It was September 1944. At the last minute the four of us were kept back, the four whose names had not been in the Party list in the captured letter. We never got to know why.

A few days later we heard that the ship had sunk. It was the 'Westphalen'. Only four were saved by Swedish fishermen.

I was shaken. My heart bled. Thirty-two drowned and ten shot, all men who had been close to me. It was all so meaningless, senseless.

Why had I been spared?

[1] 'Viking Norsemen, venture forth! Bringing strength to many others.' From a song by Grieg.

4
To Freedom

It was approaching spring 1945 when 360 of us were called out one day after roll-call. There was great anxiety in the camp. We were ordered to pack up and be ready to move off at dawn.

We were taken to a special SS camp near Mysen, a little village not far from the Swedish border, set in rolling, wooded country. The camp consisted of only three huts with very little free space around them. It was very strongly guarded.

The commandant was a high-ranking (Standartenführer) SS officer who had come from Dachau and Auschwitz to make a 'real' concentration camp in Norway. This was in order to avoid the necessity of sending Norwegian prisoners to German concentration camps in future.

Near the three huts into which we were crowded was a racecourse with open country round about. Here a full-scale concentration camp was to be built up. The commandant's first aim and interest was to get the gas chambers constructed.

One day rumours reached us that Hitler had issued orders—this was now in the last month of the war—that all political prisoners were to be shot. The Swedish border was close by. We knew that this ruthless camp commandant would not hesitate to carry out Hitler's orders and shoot us all. So there was talk of a mass escape.

News of Denmark's liberation came. Surely it would be Norway's turn soon. It was a critical moment. What was to be done?

Then a fortunate thing happened. The commandant got into some sort of a fight with his own officers. The story is that someone punched him in the eye, which turned black. He called in one of the prisoners, a Norwegian doctor who was an eye specialist. The doctor pretended the eye was in a very serious state, fussed over it, and strongly advised that the commandant go at once into a good hospital he could recommend. In his anxiety, the commandant took this advice, was packed off to hospital a long way away, and so was not there during the last critical days before our liberation.

So, after two months at Mysen, we were free.

It was late afternoon when I came home. Father and mother had got news that I was on the way. The flag was flying and the house decorated as for a festival. It was an unforgettable moment. The first few hours I was like a puppy, running all over the house from room to room, out into the garden, down into the cellar, up into the attic. Were my skis still there? Then out to the garage to have a look at our faithful Chrysler.

Flags were flying from every flagstaff in the country during these wonderful spring days. A whole nation celebrating. Men plucked straight from death met their fellows again. It was a moment in history that a people cannot expect to experience more than once.

I happened to be in Oslo the day Crown Prince Olav arrived. The news went from mouth to mouth, 'Crown Prince Olav is coming.' It seemed as if the whole of Oslo was down at the harbour to receive him. We strained our eyes to get the first glimpse of his ship. Then he was there among us amid scenes of jubilation and enthusiasm beyond description. It was not only because he was so popular but because he was the visible embodiment of the fact that we had won our freedom, that we could live again as free people.

For me, however, the great experience was to meet—Steinar! I had heard the incredible news that he was alive and then, one day in June, we ran into each other on the suburban train to Oslo. When I opened the door I caught sight of him at the other end of the carriage. He saw me. We ran and embraced one another quite oblivious of the people around.

How had it come about that he was still alive?

A few hours after he had hauled my package up to his cell window in Grini, he and his friends had been taken to Victoria Terrace. Their jackets and shoes had been removed and their wrists had been roped so that they were tied together two by two. Then they were ordered out into a lorry covered with tarpaulin, so that no one could see them. Two armed Gestapo guards were in with them. They drove out of Oslo with police cars in front and at the back. It was just before midnight.

Suddenly Steinar remembered that he still had the pocket knife his wife had smuggled in to him at Grini. Slowly and with infinite care he managed to get it out of his pocket, opened it, and, while the lorry hurtled on through the darkness, began to saw away at the rope.

Suddenly the lorry stopped. Heated voices were heard and a beam of light from the Germans' pocket torches flashed over their faces. Was this the end? But it was only that the car at the back had engine trouble. It remained by the roadside while the others drove on. Steinar continued to saw at the rope. Then he noticed something warm running down his hands. He had cut his wrist but he sawed feverishly on. At last the rope fell slack. 'Will you take a chance too?' he whispered to his comrade to whom he had been tied. But the latter had already given up hope.

At a sharp bend the lorry slackened speed, and at that moment Steinar stood up. Holding the knife with both hands he threw his full weight against the tarpaulin. There was a great rip and he tumbled out head first. He fell clear of the lorry and was up and into the woods. Brakes squealed, shouts and orders resounded. Shots rang out. He fell, tripping over a root. While he lay there he heard the engines start up again. The truck drove on to Trandum, a military training area. There, in the forest, the Norwegian prisoners were shot.

Steinar got up and groped his way forward. Soon he came to a fence and tried to climb over, but he was so spent that he had to give up and go on through the woods. Barefoot and jacketless he forced himself on step by step through the September cold. Then he saw lights from several houses. After a minute's thought he knocked on one of the doors. He was well received and was given food, clothing and money. Then he took the train to Oslo, found his wife, and the two of them made their way to Sweden.

After the liberation he went out to the place where he had succeeded in escaping. He felt again the chill of fear when he discovered that the fence he had tried to climb over had been the boundary fence of a German airforce camp! The house where he had been welcomed happened to be the centre of the Resistance in that area.

II

After the first days of celebrations were over, I began to find things difficult. Everything was different from what I had thought it would be, different from what I had pictured. I had been taken from home a youth and had come back a man, I felt. But the family received me as the boy I no longer was. I had violent reactions to the care my relatives and friends lavished on me. I wanted to avoid all that and be on my own.

It was only when I was alone up on the mountain slopes that I felt free in mind. After all I had been through I could not stand the everlasting celebrations.

So much had happened. One day I met the wife of one of the men, whose name was Peder, who had had in his home the presses for printing our illegal newspapers. He had been one of those taken to Trandum with Steinar. She came to me and said, 'When do you think Peder will be home?'

I couldn't answer.

Joy and jubilation, sorrow and loss, pride in victory and desire for revenge, did not these sweep through us all like great waves? At any rate that was how I felt.

One day shortly after the capitulation I was up at the Akershus fortress, overlooking the Oslo fjord, with several comrades of the Home Front. We had guard duty over Gestapo agents and German security personnel who were imprisoned there. A couple of us from the 'Grini Gang' were standing talking on the parade ground when we heard that a carload of prisoners-of-war had come in. British military police were escorting them and we went nearer to have a look. The Germans were in airforce uniforms and told us they were airforce officers. Then a shock went through us. There stood the hated camp commandant of Grini and his brutal special security officers—the men who had been the cause of terror and suffering to thousands. There, too, was the man who had inflicted punishment drills on one of my friends so ruthlessly that my friend died of a heart attack.

Now they stood there playing innocent. 'Airforce officers! That's the most bare-faced impudence we ever heard,' we said, as we approached them. We saw by their looks that they had recognised us. This time, however, we were the masters. So we gave them punishment drill. 'Attention! Lie down! . . . Attention! Crawl! Get on there! . . .' I made the commandant sing the same sentimental marching song, 'Marianne', that he had made us sing. 'Attention! Round and round.' They sweated. One of them begged me for water. I got hold of a bucket and threw the water in his face and all over him. My comrades laughed and were delighted.

The same afternoon I looked in on a friend nicknamed 'Hardhausen' (hard nut) to tell him about this. He was one of my room mates in Hut 10 who was now back at work in his business in Oslo. He followed intently all I said and thought it was excellent. I had done what thousands of prisoners longed to do and given these hangmen a little of what they deserved. 'Only you should have been harder on them,' he said. He seemed to be almost envying me.

I noticed that I became popular through this story, so I passed it on to all the fellow prisoners I met. Popular yes, but I wasn't happy. I had an uncomfortable feeling that there was something not quite right. One day I was going home on the train from

Oslo. The train had just stopped at Grorud when my conscience said, 'There is no excuse. What you did was rotten.'

I knew inside that it was true and I despised myself. I wanted to fight for right and justice, but this was lust for revenge. It hurts to see the naked truth about oneself. In my own nature there was the root of the same evil of which I was accusing National Socialism and the Germans.

That was the kind of battle going on in me as I walked alone through the woods. I began to understand what the professor had been talking about when we were together in Grini—to seek guidance and let one's conscience be the deciding factor in one's actions. One evening in June I was sitting quietly pondering all this up at Liabakkåsen in the wooded hills about twenty minutes from our home. I got to thinking about the Gestapo agent who had treated me worst and it suddenly came to me: 'Tell him you forgive him.' It was a thought that shocked me. Forgive a man like that! What would my friends think? Norwegian opinion was unanimous in wanting such men brought to trial and punished.

I told my mother and she, too, felt I should do it. The day I went to Akershus she came to me and said, 'Say that I am praying for him.'

When it came my turn for guard duty I summoned him and we stood face to face. He knew me and his glance was uneasy. I looked him in the eye and said the words that had come to me and added what my mother had said. He shook all over but did not say anything, and I put him back in his cell.

Later he was condemned to death and executed.

5
The Call

I

IN the autumn of 1945 I began studying for the preliminary examinations. The professor who had come to mean so much to me in Grini was now my teacher and friend. During the next years I was wholly occupied studying. Many of us had a good deal of ground to make up because of the time we had lost.

So I was often in the professor's home, where he and his wife let me come and go like one of the family. There I also got to know three other students—Inge, Aage and Jens—who became my closest comrades.

Aage was studying medicine and Inge theology. Both had been active in the Resistance, but had been able to escape to Sweden. Both returned to Norway with the police troops on liberation day. Aage was a happy soul with a bubbling sense of humour, and he found work easy, having the gift of finding his way swiftly and surely in every situation.

Inge was quite a different type, more of a thinker and rather sensitive and reserved. He had grown up amid the best of Norwegian folk art and culture and taught us to appreciate these values.

Jens was the youngest, a man full of ideas and lively temperament. He lived and breathed for the theatre and literature. We worked together on philosophy, discussed Hegel and Marx, and read Koestler.

We met frequently in the professor's home, as many as twenty to thirty of us, and many were the topics we discussed. They ranged from Jean Paul Sartre's existentialist philosophy to educational tendencies in the United States. Together we were trying to discover and understand and evaluate the lines of thought of these post-war years. We felt the need to orientate ourselves to the times we lived in.

Our common interest was how to make practical those ideas of the professor's, which had so intrigued us. We wanted to know what sort of future we would have, whether we ordinary men and women could do anything to shape circumstances or whether we were fated to be shaped by them. Had not these last bitter years taught us that it was free men, we ourselves, who must direct the course of events? Unless we did so, events would direct us. Hitler and his minions had created a Nazi ideology, mobilised a whole nation behind it, and won most of Europe. Could we not find a democratic way of life that could win nations not by force but by the power of its own moral attraction?

II

In June 1947, a large group of us students was invited to Caux in Switzerland, the headquarters of Moral Re-Armament in Europe. There in a tiny Alpine village, high in the mountains overlooking Lake Geneva, lies Mountain House.

The large building, like a fairy-tale castle against the sky, was given by the Swiss for this work. Their land had been spared from the frightful destructions of war, they said, so they wanted to create a meeting place for all the nations of the world, a place where they could find an idea that could unite all men and overcome hate and bitterness.

We had followed with keen interest the world conference that had taken place in Mountain House in 1946, and when we ourselves began our journey southwards we had great expectations as to what the trip might bring.

We were not disappointed. In Caux we met men and women from many nations, races, confessions and from every walk of life. As we got to know this cross-section of the globe and had opportunity to exchange thoughts and experiences with the different ones, a whole new world opened before us.

The thing that made the deepest impression on me was to see the transformation and change that took place in people's lives. Far-reaching change in human nature affected what seemed to be insoluble conflicts—economic and social conflicts, racial strife, and political battle. This was change forged in the hard school of daily life, bringing men to decide to stand for what is right in every circumstance of life. We heard Dr. Frank Buchman, the man who had initiated the idea of Moral Re-Armament, say: 'Human nature can be changed. That is the root of the answer. National economies can be changed. That is the fruit of the answer. World history can be changed. That is the destiny of our age.'

One day we had a meal with a head-mistress from Burma. 'Look,' she said, demonstrating with her slender hand, 'when I point my finger at you, three fingers point right back at me. It's the same when we criticise others. The difficulty in the world is that we all want to see someone else change. Nations want to see some other nation change. But everyone is waiting for the other to begin. The only place to begin is with ourselves and our own nation.'

So simple, yet so true. It was equally hard to deny the next thing she said, 'As I am so is my nation, and as my nation is so is the world.'

We had seen into the deeper roots of the conflicts that shape world history—the eternal battle between good and evil as it is fought out in me, in my country, and in the whole world. We had discussed such topics theoretically often enough as we sat in the professor's home. But here it began to dawn on me that every man is called to take a part in shaping the future. What I had met in Caux was an ideology, the positive alternative to the destructive materialism we had faced during the war. This idea was available for everyone, so simple that everyone could grasp it, so comprehensive that it could unite everyone, so compelling that it would demand everything to make it a reality. This ideology of change was able to create new men, new nations and a new world.

In spite of all the convincing things I saw and heard, however, I remained a cautious observer, benevolent but uncommitted. 'Don't jump in all at once,' I said to myself. 'It can't be as clear and simple as all that. If I stake everything while I am here, in this atmosphere and all, I might come to rue it later.' A mass of new ideas and impressions were working in me. I wanted to go home and think things through at leisure. So I returned to Norway.

A week later I went on a summer holiday with my father and mother. It was like old times. For the first time since the war we took off in the Chrysler. For some days we travelled along by the Vestlands fjords and then stopped at a hut away up by the mountains of Jotunheimen. It was a dream place. A stream ran nearby, full of trout. From the small seter (summer farm) not far away we could get all we needed. Cows grazed on the mountain slopes and the music of the bells came across the valley to us. The autumn air was clear. In the evening we would enjoy the luxury of freshly caught trout and some wonderful surprise dessert that mother had conjured up as if by magic. Then we would sit round the hearth playing ludo, reading, or talking together till we began to nod.

One day sitting by the edge of the stream watching father cast his fly, a thought came to me, quietly but with compelling clarity: 'The life you saw in Caux is the life you shall live always.' And as I sat there, I made up my mind to do so.

Every day now I began to seek God's guidance for my work. This gradually gave me a new discipline and order in carrying out the tasks I set myself. I noticed it most in my studies. I learned how to use the time effectively. There were no longer wandering thoughts or eyes but a new power of concentration.

Specially significant was the work I did on a task set us by the professor of philosophy. He had given us four themes to choose from and I had chosen 'Karl Marx and the Communist Manifesto'. It involved a great deal of quite new and unknown material and I worked hard on it for six weeks. When I was finished I read my paper to the professor and students, and at the end the professor gave his evaluation of the work. It was an experience which deepened my feeling of gratitude for the university.

I did not know then how much it would mean later that I had tried to make myself familiar with this field of thought.

III

Inge, Aage and I used to meet at the university at lunch-time every day with a number of other students who had been at Caux with us. We talked about everything under the sun, but first and foremost we exchanged experiences of the new life we had been introduced to.

One thought that came to us was to have a youth camp in the summer holidays. Many of the youth, in reaction following the tremendous tensions of the war days, were apathetic and interested in nothing. 'Would it not be possible,' we said, 'that the sense of responsibility we found at Caux could become effective for the youth here in our own country?'

We sent out invitations and at midsummer a hundred youth, both men and women, gathered for four weeks at Sjøstrand near the Oslo fjord. We conducted the whole camp ourselves. One of the aims was to get the youth from all parts of the country and from the most widely different backgrounds to learn to work together.

Every day we had two meetings for ideological instruction, when we took up themes like National Socialism's and Communism's basic ideas, how we could meet their challenge in our own minds, and what part each could have in creating in our own country the moral and spiritual climate which would make our land a fortress for democracy.

Gymnastics, swimming, football, handball were also in the

daily programme. Families and relatives visited the camp at the weekend and for them we presented the things we had learned and experienced during the week. This was often done through songs and plays. Our guests were delighted and came more than once and supported us financially. This was quite important, for we had underestimated the cost and set too low a charge per person for those taking part.

The final weekend a Cabinet minister visited the camp. He took great interest in all we told him and, at the closing meeting, spoke from his heart, underlining how essential for democracy moral standards were. He urged us to take full responsibility for the community we lived in, and said how glad he was to see what we had started.

During the Christmas holidays in 1948 many of the youth from different countries whom we had got to know in Caux, visited us in Norway. They were the same age as ourselves and were giving their whole time and energy to the work of raising moral and spiritual standards in the world. Without salary and without any compensation they were following their call. They came to Norway from England, where they had been taking part in a musical play called 'The Good Road', which had been shown for several weeks at His Majesty's Theatre, London.

Inge, Aage and I went on a skiing holiday with these young fellows and stayed at a farm in Telemark.

One evening we were sitting round the fire and they were telling us some of their experiences with such humour and such little self-concern that we burst out laughing. But in the middle of all this they said, 'One reason we came here from London was to invite you three to travel with us for a year or two—beginning now.' It was quiet for a long moment. The logs crackled on the hearth. I could hear my heart beat. It was a very uncomfortable idea. 'Laughable,' I said to myself. 'It's quite impossible. I am taking history as my second subject in the spring. Aage is two-thirds through his medicine and Inge has only one more year to go in theology. So there's no point in thinking of such a trip now. Maybe when we are through with our studies.'

Aage's deep bass broke the silence. 'Fine,' he said. 'What are we waiting for, fellows? I have had a feeling for a long time that this is right.'

The rest of us were still silent. Finally I said, 'I'll have to think it over first. I don't believe it's possible now.'

They were not easy days. I fought. I had been given a challenge which I could not evade. There was no both—and. It was either yes or no.

What would mother and father say? What about the future? Education, position, career, marriage, home—all that I had dreamed of? If I said yes, what security would I have for the future? None at all. No income. No degree which might help me to get a good post. At the same time I knew that this was not just a matter of sober human calculation. It felt like an insistent call, even if, at the beginning, I could not determine whether it was from men or from God. Finally it was clear to me that if I was to find inner certainty I had to be free of all plans for the future, free of all fear of what my friends and family might think and say.

The last night I lay awake thinking. I saw before me Olav and the others who had been taken out to Trandum. I saw those who had been lost on the 'Westphalen'—one by one they passed before me in review. I remembered the promise I had made in the hour of my deepest need in B24, that if God gave me life and freedom again, I would fully and wholly be His.

At once all doubt vanished. 'Follow me,' the inner voice said. 'Launch out. Have no fear. I will look after you.'

It was the deciding factor. I felt that no one could shake the conviction I had come to. Early the next morning I told the others.

Inge had also decided to follow the call and launch out.

When I got home father and mother welcomed me so warmly that I did not know what to do. How could I manage to tell them what I had decided?

In the evening I got mother to go to bed early so that I could see father alone. Then I told him of my decision.

Father was one of ten children. My grandfather was a shoemaker and the possibilities of advancement for so many children were not great. As a young man father had dreamt of becoming a naval officer, but he had not been able to manage it financially. So he wanted to give his only son all the opportunities that had been denied him. He worked hard so that I would be able to finish my studies without having to borrow money. More than anything else he rejoiced that I was well on the way.

Rather bent, father sat and listened to what I had to say. I could see what it was costing him. Finally he said, 'Leif, you know how much I have longed to see you complete your education and what I hoped you would become. But I will not stand in the way of your conscience. Follow your call.'

Never had I felt such devotion to my father.

It was just as hard for my mother when I told her the next morning. When she had finished weeping, she saw God's hand in it too. Then she told me about the time I was born. I had come into the world a few weeks too early. 'You were so small we could have laid you in a shoe-box,' she said. Not knowing whether I would survive, they had had me baptised at home. After that, mother had gone off by herself to pray. She had promised God that if He let me live, she would never make any demands on me as her son but would put me at God's disposal to be used in any way He saw fit.

6

A New Force

It was not easy to say goodbye to the university, to my books and the studies which had gripped my imagination and were my chief interest. It was even more difficult to leave my father and mother, especially when they felt the time would come when they might need me. I was taking up a task which offered no material security at the moment nor in the future. To many this seemed not only quite abnormal but plain madness, especially when they heard that I would have to draw out my savings, carefully deposited for my university studies, to cover my fare and living expenses. Humanly it seemed that the doors to a 'golden' future were closing.

Yet conviction grew in me with overwhelming power to go ahead, a conviction which I knew was right without the shadow of a doubt from the time I said yes to God's call when we were together in Telemark. However it took some time for this inner conviction to come to full flower and find concrete expression.

During the last two terms at the university the thought had come to me repeatedly, 'Go to Germany'. I tried to get rid of it but it kept coming back. Nor could I get rid of the thought that had come to me in B24: 'It is through total defeat that Germany will be given the chance of finding her true destiny as a nation.'

I had travelled through Germany in 1947 and it had made a deep impression. The hordes of people at every railway station, the selfish fighting for places in the overcrowded trains, the bombed-out cities, the begging children, the countless cripples, and, worst of all, the faces—lifeless, hard, crying out of ruins within—these burned into me. As I stood at the train window I often said to myself, 'A nation conquered and a land laid in ruins —what now? What millions built their faith on has failed. Where can they turn to now? What will fill the vacuum? A nation without faith and without hope will perish. Who will give them something new and true to live for?'

I used to talk to the professor about it and I was frequently in his office at the university. Among other things he told me what Frank Buchman had said at the opening of the first World Assembly at Caux in 1946. Dr. Buchman had looked out over the huge gathering and had asked, 'Where are the Germans? We cannot build a new Europe without Germany.' So the Germans had been invited to Caux together with people from all the other nations.

Obviously something had begun to happen in Germany. A little book came into my hands called 'Es muss alles anders werden' ('Everything's got to be different') which had been written by a group of German political men, trade-union leaders and journalists, who wanted to pass on to their fellow countrymen the experiences and ideas they themselves had discovered in Caux. It was easy to read, attractive, and a challenge to everyone to take part in building true democracy in Germany. It said that 'everything *can* be different'—provided that the individual, the average John Smith, experiences far-reaching change, and lives out in his own daily life the basic ideas upon which justice and freedom rest. The paper needed for printing 'Es muss alles anders werden' was a gift from Sweden, from people who wanted to have a part in creating a new philosophy of life in Germany. This made it possible to publish and distribute an edition of one million copies throughout the country.

One day I heard that a group of leading Germans had got in touch with the Moral Re-Armament force in Caux and asked them to come to Germany with 'The Good Road'. Eagerly we followed the news of their tour, 250 people travelling the country from south to north, as the reports came in from Ulm, Munich, Stuttgart, Frankfurt, Düsseldorf and Essen. The theatres in each city were crowded out. Men and women came, sceptical, yet looking for something. Many stayed after the performances and gathered back stage to talk with the actors. I had seen the play when I was in Caux and I knew that it dramatised for the Germans ideas that could lead them on the way towards responsible freedom. I heard that a member of the government of Hesse had frankly said to one of my friends who was in the play, 'For many years the German people have praised, supported and defended a political illusion. The result has been endless suffering for Europe and the world and the guilt is Germany's. We shall only save our land by bringing up our youth in a new spirit. Germany needs Moral Re-Armament as the basis for her democracy.' His wife had lost her life at the hands of the Gestapo.

I took a lively interest in all the news that came and I had the feeling that when I had finished my studies I would go to Germany to help build something new.

At that time I was constantly getting letters from Jens, who was travelling with 'The Good Road' play and wrote to me about the people they were meeting and all that was happening. He and others had remained in the Ruhr after the performances in Essen and Düsseldorf were over and he wrote that the government of North Rhine-Westphalia had asked them to remain 'to spread the message and spirit of Caux in our land and thereby help our people to find new hope and strength'. On the initiative of one of the ministers in the government, another play, 'The Forgotten Factor', was translated into German and rehearsed with a German cast. The première took place in Essen at the Kapitol Theatre which, according to Jens, 'stood out amid the ruins of the huge Krupp factories'. The play was then put on all through the Ruhr.

Just as this Ruhr trip was coming to an end, Inge, Aage and I came home from our Christmas trip in Telemark. Aage had decided to go to Caux. I was clear where I wanted to go—to Germany. It was not so simple for my mother and father however.

Relatives and friends thought it was senseless to 'waste his time on the Germans'. Others shook their heads, 'Remarkable what an interest he has in Germany!' After I had gone a few whispered that I had 'gone over to the enemy' and had 'betrayed Norwegian interests'.

However, Inge and I set out. It was early spring of 1949.

In one of the Rhine cities we were able to see a performance of 'The Forgotten Factor'. It had been played in a whole series of towns, first in the Ruhr and then in the Rhineland, and 140,000 people had seen it.

The play centres round the conflict in a vital industry between the hard-hearted director, Wilson, and the equally hard-boiled union leader, Rankin, who are at daggers drawn. The situation has grown so bad that violent clash seems imminent. Negative forces are at work to use the bitterness of both sides. The villain of the piece, Joe Bush, is out to use the workers in an uprising aimed to take over power.

When the curtain rises, we are in the home of Wilson, the director, early in the morning. Wilson is clearly in a bad humour, worried and occupied by difficulties at the plant, demands from the shareholders, differences with his board, under pressure from government regulations requiring increased production, and threats of strike action from the men. He divides his time between reading the newspaper and quarrelling with his wife. She is equally occupied with her ladies' teas, gossip, meetings, shopping, and so on. The daughter floats around with just one idea in her head—the part she is playing in her school play. Finally the son comes sneaking in the front door, for he has been out on a binge and has wrecked his father's car. This is the Wilson family breakfast.

Next we see the union leader's home the same morning. Mrs. Rankin, the wife, badly dressed and with ragged slippers, has just finished laying the table. The son comes home from his newspaper round. Mother and son are talking together when they are interrupted by Joe Bush, who comes in to get Rankin to break off negotiations and lead the men out on strike. Bush's aim is to get himself in as the leader of the men, so he is trying to weaken Rankin's position and create division around him, and even to sow suspicions about her husband in Mrs. Rankin's mind. Rankin's one aim is the working classes' fight. He is an idealist. The cause must take first place. The family, wife, son and daughter, must take second place. News comes that the situation at the factory has grown more acute. Police have arrived with weapons and tear gas. It seems impossible that anything will bring the two sides together now.

But something unexpected happens to the chief characters. There is a friendship between the daughters of the two families. Even more important, the director's son has met people who have opened his eyes and altered his thinking. He realises that he, too, is responsible for the factory, for the workers and their situation, for his father's difficult position, for the union leader's battle, and for the disastrous consequences of a strike for the whole country. What might be the way out of the deadlock so that both sides could meet as men—men who needed one another? Quite against all normal procedure young Wilson goes to Rankin's home. He is thrown out but persists, and finally gets in and wins understanding.

The action reaches its dramatic highpoint in the director's home. Rankin comes to him there to try and build the basis of a solution to the conflict, but is coldly rebuffed by Wilson. But Wilson's family have seen that a new way must be tried, so the wife, daughter and son ask Rankin to stay on. They realise that the lack of confidence between the two men must be overcome. A great battle goes on inside the director. At that moment heated voices are heard outside, and Joe Bush and a big crowd of workers burst into the house, creating a storm of bitterness and hate. The workers are astonished to find Rankin in Wilson's home and Bush insinuates, 'How much is Wilson paying you to keep the men in line?' After a violent to-and-fro Rankin makes it clear to the workers that this affects not only them but the whole country. 'It's not a question of who is right, but what is right.' Gradually Joe Bush loses ground, not having any constructive programme. When Rankin guarantees to secure a fair and just settlement for the workers and to lay the proposals before them at the union meeting in the evening, he carries the majority of the men with him. Wilson sees that Rankin really can be trusted. The two men sit down to work out a settlement together and the audience know that they are on the way to discovering 'the forgotten factor'.

The play made a deep impression on me and I could see it moved the rest of the audience similarly. How was it that it had such an effect that some left the theatre in anger while others stayed on to talk and discuss, to learn more and begin to find a new direction for their lives?

Was the secret that each person on the stage was filled with a burning conviction that he was a humble servant of the message he was giving? Those in the cast included a clergyman, an army officer, an agricultural student, a nurse, an artist, a housewife. For each one, taking a part in the play had meant a break with their accustomed ways and a surrender of material security. This courage and daring shone through their acting. This was theatre as a weapon, a play with a programme. The same conviction was also the mark of the songs sung by an international chorus of youth who travelled with the play. After the final curtain speakers from many countries told from the stage how the play's basic ideas had worked out in their own lives.

What had perhaps the greatest effect was the play's fundamental idea—people can be different, can receive inspiration and break out of the hopeless circle of circumstance. That creates something new. An ordinary young man is given vision. He lives it out. In this way he becomes an instrument in turning the tide. For at the heart of problems big and small are people and the kind of life they lead both privately and publicly. The audience were given hope that each one has a part. As the international chorus sang:

'Empty hands and empty spirit—
Change must come across the nation.
Out of bitterness and sorrow
Springs today a liberation,
Men made new in heart and spirit—
Change can come across the nation.'

That evening in the City Theatre a woman spoke, whom I got to know in the days that followed. She was Irène Laure, a member of the French Chamber of Deputies, representing her home city of Marseilles. For many years she had been the secretary of the Socialist Women of France. As an active leader in the Resistance she had had to endure great suffering at the hands of the Gestapo. They had even once tortured her son, thinking to force her into telling all she knew. She kept silent. 'I only had one wish,' she told me, 'and that was to destroy all Germans.' Yet now she and her husband were travelling in Germany with 'The Forgotten Factor'. They lived in German homes. Irène Laure talked to millions over the German radio stations. She talked in the Land Parliaments, to the trade unions, and, every evening after the play, from the stage. I could not help admiring her. She was not tall, rather pale and thin, calm and quiet in her manner. But when she began to speak she possessed such power of conviction that it commanded attention. 'Can you picture to yourself what it meant for me to come to Germany? I am a mother and a grandmother. I am a Socialist and all my life I have talked about brotherhood, yet in my heart I have wanted all these ruins. I must ask forgiveness for my hatred from you people who lived in these ruins.

'It is not that I forget the ruins in my own country or in the other countries. By no means. But what I can do is to admit the hate in me and ask forgiveness for that. Moral Re-Armament is the strongest force working to create unity between our two peoples. A common ideology for France and Germany is doing today what sentimentality was never able to do between the two wars.'

Another person I met that evening in the Stadttheater was Peter Petersen. He was one of the Germans taking part in the play. He was about my own age, rather tall and slim. He was fair-haired, had clean-cut features, and moved alertly and with a certain air of discipline. I helped him to put away the props and clear up the stage, after the crowds had left the theatre. I could not help liking him, although his appearance and manner reminded me somewhat of the German officer who had tried to convince me so enthusiastically of the superiority of National Socialism that day in Møller Street 19. But there was a marked difference. Peter Petersen's look had a calmness and a friendliness that spoke of some deep inner change.

A day or two later I drove north from Coblenz with Peter, on the way to North Rhine-Westphalia. I cannot remember how we got to talking about the war days, but in the course of conversation I got a vivid picture of all he had been through.

I discovered that, while I had been fighting my battle in cell B24, he had been living through the first thousand-bomber raid of the war, a nightmare affair that spread flaming destruction through his native city, Hamburg, and which strewed hundreds upon hundreds of burned and charred corpses through its streets and squares. For the first time in his life he heard fellow Germans curse Hitler.

Peter had never known anything else but the Hitler régime. 'I never knew what democracy was until I met MRA,' he said. Next door to the Petersen home was a place where the Hitler Youth met. They had a band. He could play the flute and liked to march up and down with the band. So, though he was only seven, they took him in. At the age of twelve he was chosen, among others, to go to the National Political Training Institute, a high school whose aim was to train up the future leaders of the Third Reich. When he was fifteen he and other boys were already helping to handle ammunition for anti-aircraft batteries, and at seventeen he was taken into the German Army. After a year or more's training, he was sent to the Western front just as the

German armies were in full retreat. In April 1945 he was wounded near Bremen. As he was convalescing, news of the capitulation came. His whole world had collapsed. There was nothing left except to go out and get drunk.

He came home to Hamburg—or what was left of it—in July. His father was a lawyer and Peter would have liked to study law, but a regulation of the occupying authorities prohibited anyone with a background like his from entering the university at that time. He might have got a job with an uncle who was in the herring business, but he could not bear the thought of smelling of fish, in addition to having no previous training for business.

In those days it was easy to denounce people as Nazis, whether they had committed any crimes or not. Peter still believed that National Socialism had been right on many points. The Western Allies would soon be fighting the Communists, he thought. With millions in Germany now trying to prove that they had never even heard of National Socialism, this was not a popular attitude and Peter's name appeared on a list of suspects handed to the British. So he soon found himself in jail, guarded by British soldiers. Every day he would ask what the charges against him were, but got no answer. After a few weeks he was suddenly released.

These experiences did nothing to change his convictions. They only made him determined to be more careful in future and keep his mouth shut. Cynical, lonely and bitter, he had nothing to live for.

Just then, however, Peter happened to meet a German family who were not cynical or despondent. On the contrary, they were on fire to take responsibility for the past and devote their energies to building something new in Germany for the future. This family had met Moral Re-Armament before the war and when, during the war years, MRA was banned and persecuted by Himmler and his men, they continued to live the life underground. Now they were planning a gathering in the south of Germany and they invited Peter. So he went. For the first time he met people whose lives challenged him to face the authority of God and what was morally right. Peter's life had been one of taking orders from human authority. Now he learned to listen to the voice of conscience and be responsible for his own conduct. The thoughts that came led to real honesty with his father. The whole family responded to his new attitude, though many of his former friends would have nothing more to do with him. Some months later, the Allied authorities gave permission for 150 Germans to go to the World Assembly in Caux, and Peter was one of those who went.

At this point in Peter's story we stopped at a parking place just off the autobahn somewhere between Cologne and Solingen. Our car incidentally, a small Standard, had been given for this work in Germany by a group of about a hundred English school-teachers at considerable sacrifice to themselves. The food we had with us came in the same way from friends abroad—corned beef from England, butter from Denmark, dried prunes and apricots from Canada.

It was good to get out and stretch and picnic there by the auto-bahn. We spread out some paper to sit on, enjoying the fresh, green colour everywhere and the scents of spring. In the distance we could see the twin spires of Cologne Cathedral pointing up towards the sky.

Eager to know what had happened to Peter in Caux, I asked him to go on with his story.

'Well,' he said, 'ever since the age of seven I had been in a uni-form of some sort, so, at the end of the war, I had no civilian suit of my own. I arrived in Caux in an old suit of my grand-father's. It was too short in some places and too wide in others. My army coat I had dyed black so it was not too bad.

'I arrived in Caux with very mixed feelings. I fully expected to hear people say, "What are these criminals, these Germans, do-ing here?" I was ready with counter accusations to whatever we were accused of. Instead, we were really made welcome. A French chorus sang, in German, a song expressing Germany's true destiny. Every door was open to us. We were completely disarmed.

'Three days after my arrival I learned of the presence in Caux of Madame Laure. I also learned that she had wanted to leave when she saw us Germans arriving. A violent discussion broke out among us. The question of guilt and who was to blame, the question that was so dividing Germany at that time, could no longer be avoided. We all recognised that this Frenchwoman had a right to hate us, but we decided that if she expressed her hatred we would reply with stories of the French occupation in the Black Forest.

'A week later Madame Laure asked to speak at one of the major sessions of the Assembly. We took seats at the back, very ill at ease and asking ourselves if we had not better leave the hall. Madame Laure's speech was only three sentences long. But these three sentences marked a turning point in our lives, as individuals, and as Germans. She said, "I hated Germany so much that I would have liked to see it erased from the map of Europe. But I have seen here that my hatred was wrong. I would like to ask all the Germans present to forgive me."

'She sat down. I was flabbergasted. For several nights I could not sleep. My whole past was in revolt against the courage of this woman. I suddenly realised that there were things for which we, as individuals and as nations, could never make restitution. Yet we knew, my friends and I, that she had shown us the only way open if Germany was to play a part in the reconstruction of Europe. The basis of a new Europe would have to be forgiveness, as Madame Laure had shown us.

'One day we told her how sorry we were and how ashamed we were for all the things she and her people had had to suffer through our fault, and we promised her that we would now devote our lives to work that such things would never again happen anywhere.'

I was much stirred by Peter's story. Later I told him of the things I had done to the Germans at the Akershus Fortress after the liberation. It was amazing how simple honesty completely united us.

Germans like Peter Petersen, women like Irène Laure, British Members of Parliament, Welsh miners, a Swiss professor, an Australian carpenter, a Canadian engineer, youth from Scandinavia, a Dutch business man—people like that were forged into a unity to fight for Germany. They used plays, a chorus, films. Inge and I became a part of that force.

We lived in Düsseldorf with about fifteen others. The Government of North Rhine-Westphalia gave us the use of offices in their building, the Haus der Landesregierung, and from there the group of us worked with German men and women who had been gripped by the ideas of Moral Re-Armament and wanted our help in spreading them.

North Rhine-Westphalia is the largest of the provinces making up West Germany. In area it is about the same as Finmark (in the north of Norway) and has a population four-and-a-half times as big as Norway. Its heart is the Ruhr. From Sieger Bergland in the south-east the Ruhr river comes flowing down pleasant valleys and then on through the industrial area to which it has given its name. Further west it meets the Rhine, that most European of rivers with its hundreds of German, French, Swiss and Dutch motor vessels and barges tugging their heavy loads upstream.

Where the Ruhr flows into the Rhine a series of large harbour basins have been built, able to accommodate the barges and motor ships, making Duisburg-Ruhrort the biggest inland harbour in Europe. If you come by car along the west side of the Rhine and look towards the other bank, a panorama unfolds that will take your breath away. Side by side, factory chimneys and pit shaft towers reach towards the sky and stretch away as far as the eye can see, while the furnaces throw up flames twenty to thirty yards high, accompanied by sparks and fireworks that illuminate the whole plant. One feels the pulse beat of Europe's heaviest concentration of industry.

If you drive into the labyrinth of streets and roads, often blocked by heavy lorries, you are swallowed up in the Ruhr's twenty-four-hour working day. One hears the ring of the heavy miners' boots as the crowds come tramping over the cobbles. They are tired and walk with the characteristic bend at the knee. They are on the way home from their shift to thousands of small, old brick houses, black with coal dust, or to the giant blocks of flats built in recent years.

Half a million of these miners burrow down nearly a mile under the ground and mine out more than a hundred million tons of coal a year—a hard and dangerous job. The same area also produces between twenty to thirty million tons of steel a year, and much of the iron ore needed for it comes to the Ruhr by ship from Narvik.

This industrial community was to be my home for the next seven years.

By reason of the results 'The Good Road' and 'The Forgotten Factor' had in the Ruhr, we soon got to know the leading men and women in the industrial, political and cultural life. The Germans took us into their homes. They shared their food rations with us, though they got very little. We slept in rooms where holes in the windows were stuffed with newspaper or rags.

We met the works committee (Betriebsrat) men in steel mills and factories. We went down the coal mines. We were guests of the different unions. Many an evening we sat round with our Germans friends discussing things while the beer mugs foamed and the tobacco smoke encircled us with blue haze.

Industrial leaders explained to us the tremendous rebuilding programme they were in the midst of. Politicians told us of the difficult problems they had to solve.

Gradually we began to understand what people's deepest feelings were in these first years after the collapse. The breakdown of Nazism had led to unbelievable misery both material and spiritual. A large part of the industries was destroyed. Hundreds of thousands of homes were in ruins. Confusion, emptiness and despair reigned. Not infrequently we discovered deep-rooted cynicism. After so many bitter disillusionments, many had nothing but scepticism left for anything from Allied sources. Among the young people especially, I often came across an attitude marked by indifference or boundless self concern. Their motto was, 'Ohne mich'—'Count me out'. But behind the wall of indifference I could see a deep longing for something new, for something to which they could wholeheartedly devote themselves, for something on which they could rely.

Sometimes we met Germans who had been in Norway with the occupation troops. It was hard to listen to an excited voice, 'Ah, Sie sind aus Norwegen! Ich war vier Jahre dort. Das war wunderbar! Ich habe Norwegen sehr gern gehabt!' ('Oh, you are from Norway. I was four years there. It was wonderful. I liked Norway very much.') When they added some words in Norwegian, like 'Nice girl! I love you!' to show that they had not forgotten all they had learnt, I would boil inside and all the strong feelings of the occupation days would come over me again. But what was the use of being furious? I had to admit my friends were right—if you see that a person or a nation needs to change the only logical thing is to give everything to inspire him to change. It was clear that a new Germany could only come about through a new type of German. That meant loving them so that they would find the will to live and build their country in such a way as to win the trust and friendship of their neighbours.

With that aim in mind we put all we had into the battle for Germany's men and women. We were led into the lives of people in a way that opened our eyes to a Germany we had not known before.

I met it first in a trade union leader. When he heard I had been in a concentration camp, he told us about the battle he and his friends had put up against Nazism. For over an hour we listened to stories of their desperate resistance. 'If we had only stood together,' he said, 'and if the democracies in the West had fought with us, Hitler would never have been able to do what he did.' He himself had been in prison for eight years—right from 1933. Physically he was a wreck, but he had an unquenchable fighting spirit and was determined to realise the vision one of his Resistance friends had given him before being executed—'Stay united and rebuild!'

I met Kurt Schumacher. He had been ten years in a concentration camp and had been so mistreated there that he had to have an arm and a leg amputated. He later lost his sight. I visited the widow of Julius Leber, the Socialist member of Parliament who, together with Wilhelm Leuschner, was leader of the Resistance movement of the Socialist Party and the trade unions. After the unsuccessful attempt on Hitler's life on the 20th of July 1944 they were both hanged, together with hundreds of others. I met one industrialist whose five brothers had all been executed. I learned about the sufferings thousands had gone through since Hitler's taking over power in 1933, and every time it raised for me the question—Have not these men and women suffered more than we? Whatever the reasons were for Europe's democracies' failure to read the signs of the times in those days, these men and women had stood alone in the fight against dictatorship for many bitter years.

In these first months in Germany I began to understand that the deeper one goes, the less is it a question of German or Norwegian, Russian or American, but that we are all part of one suffering human race. It was no longer a question of holding on to my bitterness over the wrongs of the past or of basking proudly in former achievements. I only felt an inner longing to be committed, along with the Germans, to creating a whole new way of life.

Wherever we went we saw intensive efforts being made to rebuild the ruins caused by the mass bombings that had spread destruction four to five years previously. One could not help being impressed by the initiative, the creative imagination, the tireless work and the indomitable will to overcome the enormous difficulties in the way. We met it everywhere and one of us from abroad remarked one day, 'While my fellow countrymen work in order to live, these Germans seem to live in order to work.'

As I saw this impressive will to work I had to ask myself, 'In what way will this force be used? What powers will this boundless energy come to serve? Or rather, what ideas will win the race to mobilise these forces for their ends?'

Little by little it became clear to me that what we were experiencing was not just a post-war era with all its complex problems and individual tragedies. Something was happening here which not only affected Germany but each one of us, a phenomenon not just concerned with the present but which would come to shape the future—the ideological war.

At the liberation in 1945, I, like so many others, thought that lasting peace had come—peace and a happy future. I had held on to that dream. The take-over in Czechoslovakia and the blockade of Berlin shook me and made me a little uncertain, but that a world-spanning, life-and-death battle for men and nations was raging, was hard to grasp while the battle was being waged without actual weapons. Not least difficult was it to understand that the war was actually going on within our democracies even while we were rejoicing over our new-won freedom and were busy rebuilding.

It was the Ruhr that made me face this harsh reality. We were in the midst of it every single day.

During these first years of rebuilding it was the coal mining industry of the Ruhr that laid the foundation for the industrial reconstruction of Germany. It was the country's life blood and the future depended on the hundreds of thousands of miners who could produce the 'black gold'.

It should be mentioned here that when the Allies occupied Germany they took over full control of heavy industry—coal, steel and iron. Their policy was one of dismantling for these industries—to break up the huge concerns to prevent concentration of big industry in the hands of any small group of men, lest thereby it might again be used by anti-democratic forces.

At the same time it soon became clear to the Allies that the industrial heart of Germany must beat if the land was to live. So they got heavy industry going under an Allied control commission. The pits, steel mills and factories began to work again. Directors were named to the big industries and the workers were allowed to organise. It was the workers more than any other group who made the new start possible. They cleared away the ruins and got the wheels turning.

The Control Commission put through a new law which permitted the forming of plant and pit committees (Betriebsräte) to look after the social and personal interests and rights of the workers. Election to these committees was held every year at first, but later it was made every other year. Every political shade of opinion could make itself felt in these committees and they came to have great importance.

Coal, as already mentioned, was the basis of the new industrial life. As we got to know the men in key positions in this important industry we discovered that an intensive battle for them was going on. It was a battle based on a world-spanning ideology and was carried on according to a plan with clear objectives. We became aware of the strength and strategy of the Communist Party.

Wherever we went in the Ruhr we found that, by and large, these works committees were dominated by Communists. Well-trained men often held the key jobs. They got help from Party comrades in the Russian-occupied zone. Together they formed a network that covered the whole coal industry. Their aim was to win control of the industry as a first step towards a planned take-over of power in West Germany.

This discovery gripped me and has occupied me ever since. It grew to a burning desire to open people's eyes to the life-and-death struggle our generation is in the midst of. What follows here can only be an outline, a few glimpses of what lies behind us and yet remains a current issue because the same battle continues day by day. On it depends nothing less than our being, or ceasing to be, free men.

7

A Greater Revolution

I

MOERS is one of the smaller mining towns on the lower Rhine. It rounds off the industrial area towards the west. It is about three-quarters of an hour by car from the Haus der Landesregierung in Düsseldorf.

In ancient times this pleasant district was settled first by the Celts and then the Romans. Today the life of the whole town is built around the Rheinpreussen Coal Company whose pits and chemical plants employ something around 18,000 men.

When 'The Forgotten Factor' was given in Moers in January 1949 we got to know two of the town's leading Communist functionaries.

One was Max Bladeck, chairman of the works committee of Rheinpreussen Pit No. 4. He was small in stature but fiery in character yet with a friendly glint in his eye. He was a clever Party strategist and had been a Communist for twenty-five years. For several years he had represented Moers in the Party's provincial (North Rhine-Westphalia) organisation. He was also a member of the union executive for the Essen–Lower Rhine district with 120,000 miners.

The other was Paul Kurowski. At first sight he seemed almost delicate, with sharply marked features. He was a dynamic personality, quite fearless and aggressive. He had been in the Party since 1922 and in that district he was regarded as one of the foremost ideologists. He was also well educated. Right after the collapse in 1945 the Party sent him to the Party school (run by the S.E.D.—the so-called 'German Unity Party') in Bad Berka in the Russian-occupied zone. On his return he was given the job of conducting ideological training for Party functionaries in the Moers district. He enjoyed the confidence not only of the Party but also of the miners, and he was on the works committee for Rheinpreussen's chemical plant.

Both Bladeck and Kurowski had been through stormy days since the Kapp coup in 1920 and the time of Rosa Luxemburg. Under the Hitler régime they had been engaged in illegal activities.

It was in the Heier Tavern on the outskirts of Moers that we had one of the first meetings with Max Bladeck. He brought along with him some of the keenest debaters in the Party. Their aim was to sink us with all hands and six of them opened fire one after the other. With passion and power they proclaimed what they believed in. The basic theme of what each of them said was —'The West European countries are preparing a new world war. Every single capitalist is a fascist at heart. The system is what must be changed. For 2,000 years Christianity has tried to build a new world—and failed. There is no ideology above class.' The 'blitz' went on for more than an hour. Then it was our turn. A Clydeside shipyard worker, a small, solidly built, energetic man, got up and his words cut through the tobacco smoke and commanded intent attention. 'The working class has never been so powerful yet has never been so divided as today,' he said. 'We have learned to split the atom but we have not learned to unite men. The workers' movement bears in itself the seeds of its own destruction unless it learns to change human nature. Human nature can be changed and it must be changed on a colossal scale. Capitalists, Americans, Englishmen must be changed. Yes, even Communists and Germans must be changed. People must be changed all over the world. Only so will a classless society come. But we don't need to wait for it till we are in our graves.'

He was followed by a worker from East London. 'Every honest man hates all the social and economic injustice that exists in the world,' he said. 'There is enough in the world for everyone's need but not for everyone's greed. If everyone cared enough and everyone shared enough, everyone would have enough. Changing the system alone is not enough. Moral Re-Armament means change in its widest sense—new social relations, new economic relations, new international relations, all based on individual change. To have a lesser aim is just reactionary.'

The next to speak was a Canadian employer. 'What has created injustices in the western world is selfishness and moral compromise in men like me. I can see how the hard-boiled materialism of the right wing is reflected in the bitter materialism of the left wing.' As the tall, slim employer disarmingly, and with many humorous touches, told the story of his own change he carried everyone with him. The meeting lasted four hours and when it broke up all were agreed about meeting again. The men came to the theatre to see 'The Forgotten Factor' and we noticed that its new ideas gripped them.

The revolutionary workers' movement in Germany was built on dogmatic Marxism and on the belief that the class war was the only way to progress. There was no other alternative. At the same time we discovered that a doubt had crept into the heart of many a good Communist, a personal conflict between theory and reality. The actual conditions in the Soviet zone of Germany and in the satellite countries made them question the very basis of their philosophy. At that decisive moment Moral Re-Armament arrived, not talking about theories and systems but appealing directly to people. Its aim was to change men's deepest motives and thereby open the way to a new and just society. So these men began to ask themselves—was it possible that there was a practical alternative to the class struggle, an alternative that was neither capitalist nor communist?

The thought that human nature could be changed was one that stuck in the minds of these men. They always wanted to hear more about it. One evening Bladeck invited Jens, who had been in the Ruhr since 'The Good Road' was given in Essen in the autumn of 1948, to come and stay with him. Jens was just the man for the job. His unquenchable fighting spirit, his quick mind, his big heart and his deep commitment to the call he had accepted—all those put him on an equal footing with these revolutionaries. Many a time Bladeck and Jens sat talking till far into the night.

At that time Paul Kurowski had gone into hospital for an operation. We often visited him in hospital and that impressed him. Obviously being cared for personally was something he was not used to. Our touches with him developed week by week, month by month, and we began to be friends.

Six months later, on a summer day in 1949, we went over to Moers to invite both couples—the Bladecks and Kurowskis—to the World Assembly in Caux.

We met in Paul and Lina Kurowski's home at Lindenstrasse 37. We went through their small garden with its few flowers, a lilac tree and four gooseberry bushes. Everything was more black than green, being covered with a layer of coal dust.

The flat consisted of two rooms and a minute kitchen—a typical miner's home. Max and Grete Bladeck were also there, together with two other couples, all members of the Party. It was pretty crowded. Five squeezed on to the sofa while I sat on a footstool.

The invitation to Caux did not come as a surprise, but we had several hours' argument before we reached a united mind. Marx, Lenin and Stalin were freely quoted and their teaching was put forward on every single point.

Yet it was clear that something was impelling them to find out some more about what lay back of this genuine friendship tha they had discovered. The one of our number who made the deepest impression on them was Geoffrey. He came from an English upper-class family, had been brought up in India and educated at Oxford. He had been all set for a diplomatic career. What had persuaded such a man to give up that kind of life in order to work day and night without salary in order to build a new world? Why was he now with them, German proletarians, with no other motive than that of serving them? It was something they had never experienced before. What was it that got people to do things like that? There must be something that went deeper than Marx's theories.

Late in the evening Paul summed up. 'Whoever refuses to live by the principles of absolute honesty, purity, unselfishness and love,' he said, 'is a traitor to his class and to his country.'

A few days later we went with Paul and Lina and the two other couples to Düsseldorf. Paul had a shiny, new, blue suitcase and they were all in their best clothes. As the train bore them southwards they began a journey which, without their realising it at the time, was to take them into a new world. A week or two later Max and Grete also set out for Caux.

In a few weeks, delegations began to come back from Caux and they had much to tell about the Bladecks and Kurowskis.

The things that they had seen and learned had caused them to revise their whole idea of Marxism. One day Paul had expressed it in this way: 'The basic theories of Marxism are outmoded. Its thought system is founded on classic German philosophy, but it does not reckon with the important and decisive fact that human nature can be changed. Class war and the tactics of class war are suicide, for it must of necessity end in world-wide war between two opposing camps and lead to total destruction.'

Soon we were able to read reports of what the two had said. Max had formulated his conclusions thus: 'Moral Re-Armament is the only ideology that does not set one man against another but shows how a man may make enemies into friends through love. In this way it is a force that fights for world peace.'

Paul summed up this World Conference in brief, telling words: 'I have sung the "Internationale" for twenty-six years with all my heart but here for the first time I have seen it lived.'

The Communist Party in the Ruhr now began to get reports that Max and Paul had come to a new way of thinking. The Party was alarmed. There were rumours that disciplinary measures were being prepared. However, what happened was something quite different. Still another Party functionary from Moers went to Caux. He was Willy Benedens, one of the Party secretaries.

Willy Benedens had a special gift of being able to grasp a situation and live into new conditions. He had been a pilot in the air force, but he tells that because of his political convictions he was put out of the air force and sent to a penal battalion which took part in the Ardennes offensive. Here a bomb blew off both his feet so that he now walks on artificial legs. But he was young and ambitious so he did not let that stop him and had already climbed a long way up the Party ladder. He was also a member of the works committee at Rheinpreussen Pit No. 5.

What happened to Benedens at Caux? Here is the story in his own words.

'When Moral Re-Armament came to Moers I attacked it as violently as I could. What surprised me was that they did not reply in kind. On the contrary they showed me care and kindness that was stronger than my hate. It made me think again. I decided I would find out what lay behind it and so I accepted the invitation to make the journey.

'In Caux I found the thing I had been fighting for through the years—a classless society. I experienced a personal change. Previously I had thought only of politics and the Party and not of my wife and children. I often quarrelled with my wife. This was the point on which my friends put their finger. They reminded me that socialism begins at home. Was I one hundred per cent socialist? I was working for peace and understanding between nations but there was war in my own home and strife between me and my neighbours.

'In Caux I learned how to build bridges between me and my fellows. Moral Re-Armament gives everyone the chance of finding the way to unity with others. It is an ideology that leads to social justice and which satisfies the deepest needs in the human heart.'

II

When Max and Paul returned to the Ruhr they went up to the Communist Party headquarters for North Rhine-Westphalia and recommended that the Party should make itself acquainted with 'Moral Re-Armament's world revolutionising idea'. They supported their opinion with quotations from Marx and Engels and made it clear that they themselves had personally decided to live a new life 'for logical and realistic reasons'. When they were turned down they sent the executive a written report, in which they gave a more detailed account of their new convictions.

Later in the summer Max and Paul were invited back to Caux, this time to take part in the closing sessions of the World Assembly. The Party forbade them to go. This they could not comply with. Their conviction, as they had expressed it in their report to the Party executive, was: 'We must do our part that the international understanding from Caux spreads to every nation. Thus we shall have done something positive for peace and for social progress.'

The West German Communist Party was faced with a dilemma. Up to now they had always followed Lenin's teaching to infiltrate every sector of society. But here were Party functionaries, hard-core men, who had gone to Caux and had themselves been 'infiltrated'. What were they to do? The North Rhine-Westphalia executive decided to use strong measures.

In September I wrote to my parents: 'In Moers we are in the midst of a decisive and exciting battle. The Communists I wrote you about have met violent opposition from their Party comrades because they are standing firm on all they saw in Caux. They are being called traitors. Things are being said behind their backs. People no longer greet them. When we saw Max and Paul yesterday they had had a summons to a Party meeting. The leaders want to take up the breach of discipline they have committed in going to Caux. It is probable that they will be expelled. We had a long quiet time together. This thought came to one of them, "I will let my conscience guide me and do what it says. It will determine my life." Paul wrote down, "A revolutionary's life is a battle. It is also a battle against the evil within oneself. Tomorrow will be a decisive day for us, for the Party and for others." '

The Party meeting next day took place in the 'Bunker', a big shelter only a stone's throw from Paul and Lina's home. It was a stormy session. The chairman of the North Rhine-Westphalia executive, Hugo Paul, was there in person. When Kurowski entered he was greeted with shouts of—'What does this spy want here?' Accusations were made against him in the most violent terms. When he tried to reply he was howled down and never managed to speak. Finally he was driven out of the room. Back home in Lindenstrasse 37 he sank down in a chair, choking. During the night Party comrades threw stones against the window shutters of his home.

In the weeks that followed Geoffrey and I went over to Moers nearly every night to be with our friends during this difficult time. The conflict of loyalties pulled them in two directions. On the one side there was the idea they had lived for for so many years. On the other was the new light that was beginning to dawn in them—an ideology more radical in its demands, more convincing in its way of life, a revolution without bloodshed. The absolute moral standards in line with which they had learned to pattern their lives and the changes this had begun to bring, not least in their relations with the Party—these were convincing experiences. The Party was making them face a moral decision. Neither of them wanted to break with the Party. They wanted to give the Party new life by creating a higher quality of living in the members. But now that they were being derided, slandered and persecuted they began to understand that the real battle line runs through each single person—through themselves and through each one of their Party comrades. That the Party leadership in practice was unwilling to recognise or apply moral principles like absolute honesty, purity, unselfishness and love, forced Max and Paul and their friends to make a choice—either to commit themselves to the truth of the new life their conscience was calling them to, or in blind obedience to follow the laid-down Party line in spite of their conscience.

We stood by them in their fight. From our own experience we knew what it cost to carry out in daily life what one knows is right. We kept them informed of Moral Re-Armament's world-wide battle as news reached us from all corners of the globe. We were one and shared with one another all the things that occupied our minds, and stirred our hearts.

It was usually late at night when we drove back to Düsseldorf. Geoffrey lived with a business man in the centre of town, while I lived with a civil servant on the other side of the Rhine. My way home led through a district where several square miles of buildings had been totally destroyed. The whole place was nothing but ruins and bomb craters. Here and there a piece of wall still stood out like a cry for help. Under the piles of rubble and rusty, twisted iron girders that poked out, uncounted bodies still lay buried. There was no light. I was surrounded by night's eerie blackness. What a world we had made—we, my generation! Our human depravity! There was another voice in me at the same time which said: 'Out of the evil night a new day will spring.' What could be more inspiring than the battle being fought by Max and Paul and their revolutionary friends? Was not this the eternal battle of mankind that every generation must wage? The battle to win freedom through moral change instead of becoming slaves under others' control? The battle to conquer the evil forces in ourselves and live in the light of truth?

On the 6th October 1949, 'Freies Volk', the official Communist Party newspaper in Düsseldorf, came out with a big article from official quarters on Moral Re-Armament. The next day it was reprinted in 'Neue Volkszeitung', the Party's organ in the Ruhr. It was written by the Party chairman for North Rhine-Westphalia and bore the title 'Unmoral Disarmament'. It was the first time the Party had openly declared its attitude to Moral Re-Armament (or MRA).

The article began by describing MRA from the Party's view-point. Then it went on: 'The dangerous activities of the MRA apostles has up to now been under-estimated by the district executives, yes, even by our Party's province executive . . .' 'MRA's work,' wrote Hugo Paul, 'has created ideological un-clarity and confusion in some of our Party units, for example in the Meerbeck–Moers district, in the Rheinpreussen pit groups, and in the Ford plant in Cologne.' After a detailed description seeking to explain the expulsion of Bladeck, Kurowski and Benedens, the Party chairman mentions the following point from a meeting of Party functionaries in Moers. The district chairman for Meerbeck described how this undermining work had already affected, as he said, a once proud district group. For months they had tried discussing matters with these comrades, but they only kept on trying to pass on this 'new ideology'.

The influence of Bladeck, Kurowski, and Benedens in Moers was already so strong that the Party had to make its directives with them in mind. Hugo Paul wrote: 'It is resolved that all comrades who seek contact with these men shall be expelled from the Party and unmasked as traitors to the workers' interests.'

After that it would have been easy to believe that our friends, from a human point of view, were crushed. With all our hearts we kept close to them in their hopes and doubts and shared the daily battle with them. We lived with them in joy and sorrow and stood by them in their decision to hold fast to what their conscience told them.

The first great test came at the elections for the works com-mittees. Everything possible was done to crush them. Every conceivable means was used to prevent their being elected. In spite of the terrific campaign against them, all three were re-elected—and with greater majorities than ever. Max was re-elected as chairman of his pit committee.

III

While this was happening in Moers a similar development had already begun in Essen, the biggest city in the Ruhr with its 600,000 inhabitants. It was perhaps also the most devastated city in the whole industrial area. It was here the Krupp family had built their industrial empire into one of the biggest in the world and during the war had employed some 160,000 men. The Krupp family residence, Villa Hügel, lay like a castle up on the ridge of the Essen–Bredeney suburb, with a view over the Ruhr valley and an artificial lake called Lake Baldeney.

But Essen is not all riches and luxury. A few miles below, in another suburb, lies the oldest part of the city called Alten-Essen. It gives one a real feeling of what poverty and misery are. Dirty, ragged children played in the backyards among trash cans and rubbish piles. Everything was black and grimy save where here and there bright green window shutters struck the eye. Towards the main street some fresh paint had been put on to brighten things up. Life must go on. On the walls were frequently to be seen big, irregular letters in red lead saying, 'Vote for the German Communist Party'.

August Metzing was a Communist and also chairman for the 12,000 miners of the Hoesch pits in Alten-Essen. He came to the première of 'The Forgotten Factor' at the Kapitol Theatre in Essen in the autumn of 1948 and it interested him. Two months later the play was given at his own mine, in the meeting hall of the Pit 'Karl'. He saw the play several times and one evening he took his wife along to see it. After the curtain fell on the last act they remained for a while in their seats looking at one another, and when they were back home in their own kitchen, his wife went straight to the point, 'What do you think about this changing? Why don't we try, August! It would be wonderful if it worked!' That evening they decided that they would begin a new life in their home.

The Metzings had been to Caux some weeks before the

Bladecks and Kurowskis made the journey. When they returned home to Alten-Essen they were most violently attacked. His pit newspaper ran a cartoon caricaturing him with a halo round his head, kneeling down to an imperialistic capitalist. Every day terms of abuse like 'traitor' and 'capitalists' lackey' circulated among the comrades.

The chief instigator of all this was Metzing's old friend, Johan Holzhäuser. They worked in the same pit and Holzhäuser was chairman of the Communist Party in Alten-Essen. What was August to do? He listened to the inner voice and the thought came to him, 'Why don't we invite Johan to Caux!'

The conversations between these two were lively to say the least, but contrary to the previous occasions, this time August did not lose his temper. When Johan furiously attacked the 'man with the halo', August only smiled and said, 'It seems to me better to have a halo round one's head than blinkers on one's eyes! Basically you've got no grounds for discussing Moral Re-Armament. You don't really know what it's all about. Go to Caux and see what the facts are. I can arrange it for you. When you have done that then we can talk some more and you can hammer me all you want. You can also report to the committee what you have seen.'

Through Metzing we now got to know Johan Holzhäuser. After peace came in 1945 he had been the one who built up the Party in Alten-Essen from zero to where it now had 1,200 members. He was a clear and logical thinker. As a speaker he could be both cutting and ironical and knew how to make the masses follow him and get them to do what he wanted. One of his hobbies was playing the accordian and we often listened to him. I can picture him still in his small living-room really giving his mind to 'Rigoletto'. Now and then he would cast a searching glance in our direction to see if we were following with interest. His wife liked to sit and knit a little in the background. Perhaps she was trying to make out what sort of people we really were.

One evening Paul and Lina Kurowski were there with us and we had some unforgettable hours together. Mrs. Holzhäuser provided coffee and sandwiches and while the wives talked with one another Geoffrey and I listened with great interest to Paul and Johan. We were struck by their mastery of the Marxist philosophy and how they could quote from one after the other of its great names. Even more impressive was the independent thinking these two miners had done. Gradually Moral Re-Armament came more and more into the conversation and then Paul and Lina told their own story of all they had seen and learned and experienced. It so gripped Johan and his wife that not long after they too went to Caux. In so doing they were quite clear what they were letting themselves in for and they made the journey in spite of warnings and threats from people in the Party.

On their return the idea spread from Johan to a member of the Party's province (North Rhine-Westphalia) executive, Alten-Essen's mayor, Herman Stoffmehl. They had known one another previously both in the Party and in the so-called Citizen's Committee on which Johan was the Communist representative and Stoffmehl the chairman. Now they met after a meeting of the Committee and sat down alone to talk. Johan told about his trip to Caux and all that had happened. Stoffmehl wanted to know more. One day in November the two of them went over to a meeting in Moers to which Bladeck, Kurowski and Benedens had invited their friends and neighbours.

The big first floor room of the 'Kroppen' restaurant was crowded out. Waiters in black and white pushed their way through the crowd and took orders for beer, coffee, cigarettes. The atmosphere was tense. A few Party men were in the audience. Had they come to make trouble or because they were seeking something new? Sitting near the wall I could see people's faces. Geoffrey and Jens were up near Max, Paul and Willy, who were all three leading the meeting. I could see that Herman Stoffmehl was listening intently.

Johan rose to speak. 'When you got the invitation to this meeting,' he began, 'I'm sure some of you thought, "Let us go and give these comrades a piece of our mind!" That's what I used to do. I thought I was always right. I have been a Communist for many years and have been well trained in the doctrine of class war. But are the Communists in Germany always right? Or are the Socialists always right? Or the Christian Democrats? Haven't we all been asking, "Who is right?" instead of "What is right?" ' The audience seemed to agree. 'I went to Caux,' Johan continued, 'and I thought, "I shall see to it that these people are unmasked!" But things went differently from what I thought. The first few days I searched around everywhere to find some hole, some point of attack, so that I could set on them properly. I examined them one after the other—capitalists, socialists, workers, trade union men, politicians, young and old. It struck me that these people were different. They had a faith and a conviction that was stronger and firmer than mine. "If you are honest," I thought to myself, "you will have to think over the consequences of this." So I did.'

A powerfully built, middle-aged miner, sitting at a table at the very back of the room, pushed his beer mug to one side. His face showed that he was drinking in every word. He leaned forward as Johan dropped his voice a little and went on: 'I asked myself, "What is class war?" It means rooting out and liquidating one class because it has failed to give humanity food and adequate living conditions. But do not we then begin to go wrong? By regarding capitalists as traitors, bloodsuckers and exploiters, fit only to be rooted out, I believe our hands will be so soiled that we shall be unable to bring any answer. It is urgently necessary to reach the men of both classes who are willing to take this new way—the right and clean way. It is absolutely possible that together we can create a situation where every man will be given his rightful place in life. Think what it would mean if a series of employers could be changed and, through us workers, find a new way of doing things! Think what it would mean if a series of us workers could be changed—for we need it too! Isn't there a capitalist hidden inside many a one of us?'

Johan made a pause. One could see him thinking. His eyes held the audience fast. They were clearly gripped. 'When we decide to give the lead by our example and live so that our country finds a faith, and make it real in daily life, then we will create a revolution without bloodshed, a revolution that knows no frontiers, a revolution of the spirit that no iron curtain, no armies or generals can stop. Our way will then be clear. It will be a reality. And it will be a clean way.'

The audience gave him warm applause.

Max was then about to close the meeting when Herman Stoffmehl suddenly got up and asked to be allowed to speak. In the sudden hush his voice sounded full of passionate seeking and strong conviction.

'I think I am the first to speak here this evening without yet being wholly convinced that the principles of Moral Re-Armament are right. I have been in the socialist movement for the last forty years and today I am a member of the Communist Party.' The audience were all ears. 'For forty years I have fought for an ideal. I have regarded scientific Marxism not just as a dogma but as a guide for all we do. I have always had the hope of seeing these ideals realised before my life's end. But when the world is overtaken by such a catastrophe as the one we have just lived through, one is forced to stop and think things over afresh. Has there been any purpose in all we have fought for? We have made the greatest economic sacrifices and staked our lives in this fight, but has there been any purpose?

'In the last few weeks I have seen a lot of my old friend, Johan Holzhäuser. We have discussed Moral Re-Armament. But I became really interested for the first time when in our Party's own newspaper I read that certain Communists, well known Moers Communists, had been expelled from the Party. I said to myself then that there must be something in this Moral Re-Armament after all. I am not one of those who blindly follow party slogans.

I have always been convinced that I have a free will. So I pounded the table and said, "This is not right". If it is bringing about the expulsion of socialists, which we all want to be, there must be something in Caux. Are they afraid of Caux? If that is the case, then that is where we belong, *that* is socialism. Moral Re-Armament is out to fight for change in existing conditions of society.'

You could have heard a pin drop. Everyone hung on the speaker's words. His voice, though not strong, was vibrant and the gestures of his hands underlined the meaning of his words. He looked like some elder statesman as he stood there tall and slim, his hair silver grey.

'They expelled my friend, Johan. A week ago I spoke for over an hour to a gathering of Party functionaries in the Stadtgarten Hall in Essen-Steele and took that up in no uncertain fashion. As a result an overwhelming majority voted with me thereafter. I have chalked it up as a point for me and now am waiting to be called before the Party presidium. I am eager to see whether they will dare to expel me, too. You may say I am rating myself too highly, but I am no anonymous Party member. I am on the province (North Rhine-Westphalia) executive and have a voice in our decisions. I will fight for my membership in the German Communist Party so that I can work within the Party for the realising of MRA's basic principles in both the Socialist Party and in the Communist Party. If you think it out you will realise that we can do much more if we remain in the Party than if they throw us out. I am going to give everything to win them to these ideas.'

He sat down. One or two of the audience hurried out, but most stayed on to talk. Late that evening we went with Stoffmehl and Holzhäuser to Paul Kurowski's, where we got a bite to eat before going on back to Essen.

A few days later Stoffmehl was at a big Party conference in the Hammacher Hall in Essen West. The meeting was chaired by Heinz Renner, vice-chairman of the West German Communist

F

Party (for the whole of the Federal Republic). The speaker of the evening was Hugo Paul, chairman of the Party for North Rhine-Westphalia. His main subject was Moral Re-Armament.

About the meeting Stoffmehl told me that Hugo Paul had finished his speech by moving the following resolution: 'No member of the German Communist Party may go to Caux. Every member of the German Communist Party is in duty bound to combat Moral Re-Armament because it is the enemy of the working class.'

After the province party chairman had finished, Stoffmehl spoke. He explained how he had come to learn about this new ideology. 'What I myself have seen and experienced,' he said, 'is for me a sign that we need to take Moral Re-Armament seriously if we are out for international peace and understanding.' Here he was interrupted by shouts and the disturbance soon developed into outright tumult. 'I was furious,' Herman told me, 'and I roared out: "Am I supposed to be talking to a rabble or to intelligent individuals?"' The chairman called for order and directed the functionaries to let Stoffmehl continue. 'We must discuss Moral Re-Armament on the broadest basis,' Herman shouted to his Party comrades. 'We must seriously take up and consider the whole question of human nature and its change.' He finished by moving the following resolution: 'We functionaries of the German Communist Party here assembled are unanimous in accepting the aim of Moral Re-Armament as a basis for discussion.'

The chairman said: 'Two resolutions have been moved—Hugo Paul's and Herman Stoffmehl's. I call for a vote.' The result was 400 for Stoffmehl, 407 for Hugo Paul.

Just before Christmas I had a letter from Herman in which he wrote, 'Unfortunately I can't meet you tonight. This is the evening when it is being decided whether I shall be expelled from the Party or not. That meeting in Moers made a deep impression on me and there is question after question on the tip of my tongue.

I hope we will have a chance to talk them over as soon as possible.'

Stoffmehl was asked to appear before a group from the Party executive. First they tried to separate him from Moral Re-Armament by showing how meaningless its ideology was as compared with the Communist ideology. When that got them nowhere they tried telling him about Paul Kurowski and what had happened to him after his return from Caux. 'He has been bribed with American gift packages, new furniture and a new carpet,' they said. 'He has been bought by the imperialists.'

But it so happened that Herman had just been in Kurowski's home. The furniture was the same old furniture. There wasn't a carpet in the whole place. And the food had been plain bread and liver spread!

Finally they offered him a city official's position in Dortmund —on condition that he write an article against Moral Re-Armament. Stoffmehl refused. A month later, the 28th of January 1950, he was expelled from the Party at a special meeting called in Essen-Steele.

The repercussions had gone far and wide inside the Communist Party in North Rhine-Westphalia. On the 8th of December 1949, the central executive had held a special meeting and a thorough-going reorganisation was set in motion, both in the central executive and in the Party secretariat on the grounds that both had been 'infected by an ideology that was at variance with the Party's'.

The 'Manchester Guardian' of the 8th of February 1950, reporting on the clean-up, had an article with the headline—'A New Communist Heresy—Moral Re-Armament'. The article went on to quote the new chairman of the North Rhine-Westphalia Communist Party executive, Josef Ledwohn, who, in his report on the clean-up, said that 'one of the most dangerous symptoms was the steadily growing contacts between Party members and Moral Re-Armament'.

Hugo Paul, the man who had expelled Bladeck, Kurowski and Benedens from the Party, had his position as chairman taken from him and also lost his place on the central executive. The charge against him was that he had not been sufficiently alert to hostile ideologies which had got into the Party's ranks.

8

'It's Different Now'

It is impossible not to like the Ruhr even with its smoke and coal dust and pouring rain, for on the sunny days that come too, one sees the green spaces and the beech trees amid the whole panorama of factory chimneys, slag heaps and blast furnaces. But its chief asset is the working people who are the heart of the whole thing.

One of the many families I came to feel very close to was the Heske family. Their home is in Essen-Schonnebeck, only a few steps from the pit where the husband, Fritz, worked. From his boyhood up he had been active in the workers' movement and he had been quite a power in the Communist Party from 1931 on. Around 1935 he was thrown into prison by the Nazis for having organised resistance against the régime, and was in prison for two years. On his release he was forbidden employment for seven years on account of his political convictions. During that time his wife, Jettchen, had to take work as a laundress in order to keep the home together. They went through difficult days. She was often unwell and suffered from dizzy turns. Once as she was going to collect her pay, she fainted on the steps of the office. The Nazi woman secretary in the office threw the money out to her with a sneering laugh, 'There you are. About all you're good for is to buy a rope and hang yourself.'

When the Hitler régime collapsed, Fritz began afresh to build up the Communist Party in his area. He also formed a cell of a hundred men at Zollverein 3/10, the pit where he was chairman of the works committee. He trained his men well and they followed his orders. For all practical purposes they had the pit under their control. In 1948 he made the trip to the People's Congress in East Berlin as the representative of the workers.

I shall never forget the afternoon we visited the Heskes for the first time. Some ten or twelve of us had been together talking over the situation facing us. More requests had come to put on 'The Forgotten Factor' again in the Ruhr and we were expecting the arrival of a cast of sixty or more people. Where were they to live? It was when we were going over the homes that had been offered and others that were possible, that someone had come up with the thought that we should perhaps ask Fritz Heske. He had come once to a Moral Re-Armament meeting in Königwinter to which the coal company had invited the works committee chairmen from the different pits. Heske had listened to the various speakers and to the international chorus from Caux and had then left without saying anything. However, we felt it was right to try and it fell to me and one of my German friends to visit Heske.

As we approached Essen-Schonnebeck, I stopped the car for a moment.

'You know,' I said to my German friend, 'I'm afraid. I feel so helpless meeting people.'

'So do I,' was the reply. 'Do you think we'll be thrown out? Heske is a powerful fellow—and very temperamental.'

'I don't know, but to be very honest I would just as soon turn round and head the other way.'

In front of us we could see the big wheels of the pithead gear at Zollverein turning. We stayed where we were and took time to tell each other what was going on inside us. We felt the need of a wisdom higher than our own. What else could we do except seek guidance? We prayed for freedom from our fears and uncertainty and that God would show us what to say. In the stillness that followed some simple clear thoughts about what we should tell the Heskes came to us. So, trusting in what had come, we drove on to their home.

We knocked on the door and there stood Mrs. Heske, an

ample, medium-tall woman in her middle fifties. We told her who we were and, smiling, she asked us in. She showed us into the living-room, a well appointed, pleasant place, and there sat Heske working at his desk.

We soon discovered that Fritz was a man who was very fond of a good chat. He and his wife listened with great interest when we told how we ourselves had met Moral Re-Armament and what it had meant to us. Fritz broke in suddenly, 'I went as the workers' representative to that information meeting in Königswinter. I liked the chorus and their clean, happy faces. Those four absolute moral standards—there's something in those.'

We got to know later that when Fritz had received the invitation to the Königswinter meeting, one of his Party comrades had said to him, 'It's not allowed to go to that. That's Moral Re-Armament.' The next day there was a message from the Party executive in Essen, 'You are forbidden to go.' His son, who had just been named to represent the 'Free German Youth' (Young Communists) at a big Whitsun gathering in East Berlin, had also attacked him, telling him he should stay at home. But Fritz had followed his own reasoning, 'Am I not the representative of the workers and should I not form my own opinion in order to be able to answer the questions the workers are always putting to me about Moral Re-Armament?'

Mrs. Heske then invited us into the kitchen, where she had biscuits and coffee ready, and the conversation went on with much humour as well as serious moments. We made fast friends that day. Just as we were going, the son came home, so we stayed on another hour. The sparks flew as we talked and we were struck by the son's clever and quick mind. He was working as an electrician with the Essen tramways.

The Heskes begged us to come and visit them again. We told Fritz that a larger group of people from abroad was coming to the Ruhr to put on the industrial drama 'The Forgotten Factor' in the Hans Sachs House in Gelsenkirchen, but that we did not know how we were going to find living quarters for them all.

Did he have any thoughts on where they could stay? 'I will help you,' said Fritz and he put on his coat and came with us. In a very short time he had got us beds and hospitality for fifteen.

A few days later we were in his home again. Fritz showed us a letter he had received from the Essen Party secretariat summoning him to a district meeting at which he was to answer for what he had done.

'There were about sixty Party comrades present,' related Fritz, 'and the secretary for the Essen area spoke. Very brusquely he laid forth the Party's opinion of Moral Re-Armament. Then he accused me of a breach of discipline and of ideological deviation. Then I was allowed to speak—not to defend myself but only to give an explanation. However, I talked for forty minutes,' Fritz went on with a smile, 'and I maintained that, as the elected representative of the workers, I must have the right to inform myself fully about a thing the workers were always coming to me with questions on. On the basis of the observations I had made, I told them that I had become convinced that these people were fighting for peace and that their four absolute moral standards were both right and necessary.'

The Party secretary repeated that Heske had broken Party discipline, but that Fritz could put it right by signing a statement rejecting Moral Re-Armament. He refused. The Party secretary then moved a resolution for his expulsion. Thirty-eight voted for, nine against, and thirteen abstained.

Heske's son had also been present. He was furious. 'What sort of comradeship is this?' he said. 'My father has sacrificed everything for the Party, his time, his energy, everything, and now at one stroke he is to be condemned and thrown out of the Party he himself has built up over these last twenty years. If that is his thanks, then I am finished with the Party too.' Thereupon Heske and his son had left the meeting. A third Party comrade demonstratively left the room with them.

On the 10th March 1950 the Party came out with its explanation in its 'Neue Volkszeitung' under the headline: 'MRA—

a Means for Preparing War.' The article said, among other things:

'For a long time Heske's conduct has given grounds for serious criticism. . . . In spite of the fact that many of his Party comrades have urgently put it to him that he should admit the errors he has committed, he said he intended to work with everyone who desired peace and, therefore, also with Moral Re-Armament. This means he will not see that Moral Re-Armament is an agent of the imperialistic warmongers for the practical preparations for war.'

At another point the article stated:

'With the agents of Moral Re-Armament one cannot hold discussions. Against them one can only wage implacable war. Therefore no decent, progressive and peace-loving person can have anything to do with these agents of American warmongers. Whoever does so, will himself become an agent and thereby places himself outside the ranks of the Party.'

The article was signed: 'For the district secretariat of the German Communist Party in Essen—Kurt Goldstein, Ernst Schmidt.'

His expulsion made a deep impression on Fritz, but at the same time it showed him that every relationship to people and ideas must be based on the fundamental values to which he had found his way. He knew well enough what went on behind the scenes in the Party and what personal battles for power went on among the Party comrades. For his son, Fritzchen, the expulsion had also been a shock and when Whitsun came, instead of going to the Youth Festival in East Berlin, he spoke at a mass meeting for Moral Re-Armament in Gelsenkirchen.

But the strongest fact in bringing a new conviction to both father and son was the change that took place in their own home. For the first time they were both completely open and honest with one another.

Things had not always been easy in the Heske home. Jettchen belonged to the evangelical church. Fritz had left the church in his twenties and had been opposed to it from then on. Party work took him more and more away from the family and when he had a meeting in his home he sent Jettchen out to the kitchen. Work for the revolution took all his interest, so he had neglected her and the love he had once felt had grown cold. For her, life had become a nightmare.

When Fritz began to apply the four moral standards to himself and began to listen to the voice within, a new life opened up. One evening a little later he came home with a great surprise for Jettchen, a concrete expression of the need he felt to restore for the past. Smiling and expectant like a small boy, he presented her with a sewing and mending basket, the lid beautifully embroidered with flowers in exquisite colours. Fritz had stopped drinking and playing poker on Saturday evenings, and had had the thought to use the money he saved to give her this gift.

A new world opened for Jettchen. Every day when Fritz came home from work he related what had happened at the pit, told her of the questions and problems there and in the works committee. When she realised that he needed her, she blossomed. His daily battle became her battle.

One day two women Party members visited Mrs. Heske. She took them into the kitchen but even in the passage they had begun to talk about Fritz. 'That rascal! You should just see how he carries on with other women and how he behaved at Party celebrations!' When Jettchen would not listen to this, they began to flatter her and asked if she wouldn't sign up as a member of the Party.

The Jettchen took the initiative and showed them a colour picture.

'What's that?' they asked.

'That is Mountain House,' she replied, 'and my husband has been there. It is the centre for Moral Re-Armament in Europe.'

Then she suggested that both women should bring their husbands to a meeting to hear all about Caux and learn for themselves what it was all about. But they shook their heads. 'No, no,' they said. 'We know what it is.' And as they left they threatened her—'Wait till the Russians come. Yes, when the Russians come . . .'

Some time later, when I was about to return to Oslo, I had a message that Jettchen wanted to see me. 'We wanted to wish you a good journey,' she said and stuck a package into my arms. I took it carefully, for it was a flower vase, one of the most precious things they possessed. 'Take it home with you,' she beamed. 'I want your mother and father to have it as a greeting from Fritz and me.'

That was the start of an exchange of letters between my mother and Jettchen that gradually developed into a warm friendship.

Christmas 1950 I spent with the Heskes. First we had a solid, miner's dinner—meat and potatoes and beans, followed by coffee and a huge plate of cake. I had to tell them how we celebrated Christmas at home, from when the Christmas tree was lit until Father Christmas had been round. After that there was a long silence, broken only by faint murmurs from the coffee pot that stood keeping warm on the shining stove.

Jettchen broke the silence. She hunted out an old Bible and read the Christmas gospel. For her it was a sacred act. Her voice faltered and the reading was shaky, but her whole heart was in it and her face shone. When she came to the end Fritz began 'Silent night, holy night' and Jettchen and Fritzchen joined in. I only listened. Jettchen's slightly metallic voice was a shade higher than Fritz's, who sang away powerfully in his own key, while Fritzchen, who had the best voice, came in somewhere in the middle. It sounded somewhat discordant, yet at the same time very natural and true. And their eyes! The eyes of people filled with a deep joy and with hearts at peace. I thought back to what Jettchen had said, 'There was a time, Leif, when I thought the sun would never shine for me again. But it's different now.' 'For thirteen years', she said, 'I have been praying to God that our family might be united again.'

Gradually the family became more and more a part of the world force working in the Ruhr. Frequently delegations came from Asia or Africa or the other continents. They came to meet the men who stood in the front line of the ideological struggle. The Heskes received many such visits and Jettchen was always the motherly hostess.

Fritz's change came as a challenge to his work-mates at the pit and some at once began to attack him. But his whole way of life had become different, and because he daily followed the thoughts that came to him in the silence, he was able to keep the initiative and make progress with the new, revolutionary idea which had gripped him.

For the first time in his life at the pit he worked unselfishly for everyone—the Socialists, the Christian Democrats, the Communists, and the politically neutral—and tried to build up a co-operation to secure the best for all.

A decisive test was the election for the works committee which came nine months after he had been at Caux. The Party organised an intensive campaign—leaflets, invented stories, slanders. Fritz took the whole thing calmly. A few days before the election he put a poster up on the notice board giving an account of the principles of Moral Re-Armament and the main lines he was trying to follow. Heske was re-elected chairman of the works committee with more votes than he had ever had before. Through his untiring fight and invincible spirit, in spite of all attacks, he won friends everywhere.

Fritz was clear that the new ideas to which he had won his way were not an ideology just for the workers. He put the same energy into creating open and honest teamwork with management too. The man he began with was a deputy manager he simply could not stand. Fritz likes to tell how it happened. 'When we went to Caux together,' he says with a faint smile, 'we were like cat and dog'. I thought he needed a lot of change but he did not seem to respond. Then suddenly one morning early the thought came to me—'Fritz, be absolutely honest and tell him what you have been doing behind his back.' You see, since the Hitler days we had been at daggers drawn. He had been a National Socialist and had made my life a misery. So after the war I said to myself—"Now it is my turn", and I began collecting material to bring a case in court against him. But in Caux the thought was very clear in my mind to stop doing this and that, together, we might find something new. We went out for a walk and on the terrace of Mountain House high above Lake Geneva I told him I wanted to drop preparing a case against him and to live in an honest relationship with him.'

From that walk, friendship began to grow. A fortnight later, back in the Ruhr, the two of them together with a few friends stood round a bonfire—a mass of papers going up in smoke and flame. It was all the material Heske had collected for the court case.

The following summer the senior manager of the mine went to Caux.

Fritz points out how little he had actually achieved through using the methods of class warfare during the years in which he thought that was the only way. But when he began to apply absolute moral standards and accepted change himself, confidence grew both inside the works committee and in their relations with management. This was to the advantage of everyone working in the pit. 'Problems will always keep coming up,' Fritz says, 'but every time we have found the way to the right solution on the basis of this new confidence.'

9
A New Thinking

IN those days when we first got to know Fritz Heske and his family, Gelsenkirchen became our most important centre in the Ruhr. This 'City of a thousand fires' lies in the heart of the industrial area. Along with its iron works, steel works, chemical plants and coal mining, it has a population of 400,000. Thirteen big pits with some sixty to seventy shafts form the basis of the city's economic life. With a centre right in this mining and industrial area we could save over a hundred miles' driving a day. So some of us, including Jens and myself, moved from Düsseldorf to Gelsenkirchen.

How we got this centre was largely due to August Metzing and his wife. In the summer of 1949 they were both in Caux. One day this old exponent of the class war spoke to the assembly. Among others on the platform sat the general manager of the biggest coal mining company in the Ruhr. Metzing finished his talk by saying, 'Here sits the Ruhr's most reactionary employer.' Then, turning to the general manager, he went on, 'But I am willing to work together with him on the basis of change and of these four moral principles.' With that he reached out his hand to the employer. They got to know one another and August suggested to the general manager that he should encourage his managers and representatives of the workers to visit Caux. This was done.

The Gelsenkirchen Coal Company, known widely by its initials G.B.A.G., employs about 90,000 men and has mines throughout the whole industrial area. It falls into four sections represented roughly by the four cities of Gelsenkirchen, Dortmund, Bochum and Duisburg-Hamborn. The administrative headquarters co-ordinating these sections is located in Essen.

The manager of the company in Gelsenkirchen and many of the workers' representatives were so impressed by what they saw in Caux that they invited 'The Forgotten Factor' to the city. The play was given in the Hans Sachs House, the main centre for conferences, concerts and plays for the whole area, and it was shown for several weeks. More than 25,000 men and women from industry came to the performances and we got to know many of them. We were asked to stay on in Gelsenkirchen and the coal company put offices, a meeting room and bedrooms freely at Moral Re-Armament's disposal. I myself was invited to stay with one of the founders of the Communist Party in Wattenscheid, a neighbouring town to Gelsenkirchen. Jens lived with the chairman of the central works committee for the company's 25,000 men of the Gelsenkirchen area.

In the spring of 1950 a number of prominent Germans asked Moral Re-Armament to hold a conference in the Ruhr. The German Chancellor, Konrad Adenauer, wrote to Dr. Frank Buchman:

'Moral Re-Armament has become a household word in post-war Germany. I think of the great success which has been achieved with "The Forgotten Factor" in the Ruhr. Through that, wide circles of men in politics, in industry, and in the trade unions have come in contact with the ideas of Moral Re-Armament. In addition, countless leading politicians, leaders in the trade union movement, in industry and in business have been invited to take part in the yearly conferences in Caux. They are grateful that Caux has given them the opportunity of discussing Germany's burning problems, on a world basis and in an atmosphere of cordial co-operation, with representatives from every country where individual and personal freedom is still preserved. I believe that in view of the offensive of totalitarian ideas in the East, the Federal Republic, and within it the Ruhr, is the given platform for a demonstration of the idea of Moral Re-Armament.'

This conference opened with a mass meeting in Hans Sachs House, Gelsenkirchen, Whitsun 1950. During this same time the 'Free German Youth' had gathered thousands of young Communists in East Berlin.

The hall in the Hans Sachs House is supposed to hold some 2,000, but on this occasion there must have been many hundreds more squeezed in. Miners, steelworkers, leaders of industry and politics, people from all parts of the Ruhr and from all over Germany were there. A group of men and women from the Russian-occupied zone had risked coming across the border and making the long journey in order to attend. Among the many representatives from some twenty-four other nations was the widow of Burma's first Prime Minister, Aung San; the chairman of the million strong Japanese railways workers, Etsuo Kato; Irène Laure; and the elderly Senator Theodore Green, one of Roosevelt's close colleagues.

The press called the meeting the most international gathering Gelsenkirchen had ever seen.

On the platform sat the men who, more than any others, had prepared the way for such a meeting—Max Bladeck, Paul Kurowski, Willy Benedens, Johan Holzhäuser and Herman Stoffmehl. With them sat also a group of youth and a number of leading industrialists whose new attitude had become the talk of the Ruhr.

The main speech was given by the man who had inspired this new thinking in so many nations. Its title—'The Destiny of East and West'. From 6 p.m. to 7 p.m. all the West German radio stations carried Dr. Buchman's words to the millions.

'Marxists are finding a new thinking in a day of crisis,' he said. 'The class struggle is being superseded. Management and labour are beginning to live the positive alternative to class war. Is change for all the one basis of unity for all? Can Marxists be changed? Can they have this new thinking? Can Marxists pave the way for a greater ideology? Why not? They have always been open to new things. They have been forerunners. They will go to prison for their belief. They will die for their belief. Why should they not be the ones to live for this superior thinking?'

The huge gathering sat spellbound as they realised how far Frank Buchman's vision had already become a reality in the shape of the powerful row of trained, convinced revolutionaries who stood up and committed themselves to this new idea—Bladeck, Kurowski, Benedens, Holzhäuser, Stoffmehl. From where I sat on the platform I could see people's faces and see how their attention was riveted.

'Is it possible to build a new world?' Stoffmehl asked. 'We answer—Yes! From the depths of our hearts we answer—Yes! For through Moral Re-Armament's four basic principles we have found something that is new in the world. It is possible that some may say this is old stuff, that these are the same ethical values which Christianity and Socialism build on. But these basic principles have not been followed and lived out and that is the decisive element. That is why we say when men change then conditions change. Because we are absolutely convinced of this. We are fighting together with those who stand with Frank Buchman, and we are fighting with the same passion as we used to fight for our previous ideas,' the speaker went on with both arms outstretched to the audience. 'Workers, employers, politicians—fight with us! Decide to change! Do not deceive yourselves that this is easy. It is very difficult. It costs a lot to apologise. But once you have done it, the way opens up.

'This is our ringing call to every man,' he concluded. 'Fight with us for a new world! Fight for the world that we all want, a world where we can live in peace and well-being, a world where there shall be no more war.'

The leaders of industry made a similar impression as they committed themselves to work together with these former Communists in order to find new methods and new aims for industry. Both parties were firm in the conviction that changing Communists and capitalists gives hope of a unity that includes everyone.

The audience were equally gripped by the fire and passion of the youth who spoke. One was young Fritzchen Heske, who was to have been an Essen representative at the Youth Festival in East Berlin. Another was the son of the G.B.A.G. manager in Gelsenkirchen. A third was the son of the Minister President of North Rhine-Westphalia.

The meeting went on for three hours. Even then there were many hundreds of people who did not want to leave, and they clustered round the platform seeking to learn more.

'Unity is our one hope,' said Dr. Buchman. 'It is the true destiny of France and of Germany today. It is the destiny of East and West. The alternative is divide and die. Moral Re-Armament offers the world the last chance for every nation to change and survive, to unite and live.'

10

Moscow Takes Notice

ONE family who were in the packed hall of the Hans Sachs House that Whitsun afternoon were the Wegerhofs. Willy Wegerhof had been for years electrician at the Holland Mine in Gelsenkirchen-Wattenscheid. He and his wife had been through hard times and many a bitter fight to keep the family alive. He was one of the founders of the Communist Party in his town.

The first time I met him was at a gathering of the works committee in the Holland Mine's canteen. Four of us had gone along to meet the committee—a Canadian engineer, a pharmacist from the Isle of Man, a big landowning farmer from Finland, and myself. We sat around the long table and were served goulash and apple juice or beer.

The works committee were a lively crowd. Wegerhof sat in the middle. I noticed his brown eyes observing us keenly with a sort of a twinkle at times. His bald head turned to follow each of us as we spoke to them. He was an outgoing type of man with a great sense of humour, and at appropriate moments he would crack a joke in a loud voice. While they all listened to us with keen interest, one could also feel that they were not a little suspicious.

The man who really riveted their attention was the Finnish landowner. He was over six feet tall and as broad as a door. When he rose he towered over the table like a huge, powerful Finnish bear. His deep voice shot out his sentences strongly in deliberate German, and he waved his arms frequently to underline his convictions. He was a remarkable sight.

'There was always trouble on my farm between the workers and me,' he said. 'Actually, I was a dictator. I was the one who decided about wages, working conditions and everything else. Anyone who did not agree with me could go elsewhere. Naturally I detested trade unions and forbade the workers to have anything to do with them.

'You can imagine,' he went on, lowering his voice dramatically, 'that it was not easy for me to change my ways. It is an amazing thing this secret of listening and letting God tell you what to do. It was clear to me at once that I must stop treating the workers as cogs in a machine. I have to admit to you that before I learned to listen I was more worried when something went wrong with the tractor than if one of the men broke a leg. But when I listened I wrote down these thoughts, "People matter more than things. Treat the workers first and foremost as people and partners."

'What this meant gradually became clear to me step by step the more I thought about it. It meant giving the men real responsibility and working out practical plans to make them co-partners in the farm with me. I decided to open up the books and financial records of the farm for full inspection by the workers and by their responsible union officials. I decided to give each worker land on which he could build his own house. I also helped him raise the money for the building and supplied him with cheap lumber and transport from the resources of the farm. Finally I decided to plan the whole running of the farm with the workers and no longer just on my own.

'When I put these proposals to the men it was such a shock to them that they turned it down point blank without giving any reasons. They just did not trust me. I think they felt it was another scheme of the boss to raise output. For several months I tried to explain it to them and get them interested in the idea but without success.

'What was I to do? The thought came to me in quiet, "Go and ask for the help of the Agricultural Workers' Union in Helsinki". I did that and the union, who could hardly believe it either, arranged for one of their organisers and his family, together with a woman cowhand trained in union principles, to come and stay at my farm. They went into the whole proposition thoroughly, and gradually the workers realised that I was genuinely determined to be different and wanted things to be better for them.

'So we tried it out. Every morning now we have a meeting to plan the work together and deal with any problems that have come up. There is a sense of teamwork and openness we have never had before, and everyone takes responsibility for the farm. One interesting point is that the cows began to give more milk. When I stopped bullying and kicking my farm folk, they stopped doing the same to the cows.' Here the tall Finn gave a vivid demonstration with his foot of how, copying him, the men had kicked the cows. The miners roared appreciatively. 'Before these changes,' the Finnish landowner went on after the laughter had died down, 'the workers' children used to run away when they saw me coming. Now they run to me as they would to their own grandfather.'

When he sat down there was much applause and some discussion. The miners were impressed with the practical realities of this story and knew it made sense. They wondered if it would work in big industry, however, in the mines and the factories. They wondered if it would work on a world scale.

The big Finn got up again. 'The problem always is how to work together and how to work effectively,' he said. 'That depends on human relations and it has to start with a change of attitude on the part of both management and labour. The only place one can start is with oneself and one's own attitude. For myself, I have decided that as long as I work my land, people will come first. I am here in the Ruhr now because I want to make our experiences in Finland available to everyone. This is a revolution that goes from man to man. My workers are behind me. They are running the farm to make it possible for me to fight for this new way in other countries. That's what they want. Workers have often been the spearhead of revolution. Why should not employers and landowners take the lead for once and give an example? I am convinced that this is the right way. Suppose everyone cared enough and shared enough—wouldn't everyone have enough? Care brings out the greatness in each man so that each can play his full part. This is a revolution of the heart which we could all live together.'

We stayed on talking to the miners for a long time. That evening we became good friends and later Wegerhof invited me to come and stay in their home.

He and his wife had four children. The eldest, Robert, who was about my own age, had been a prisoner of war for five years in Russia. I was given his room and Mrs. Wegerhof looked after me like a son. Every morning there would be small, fresh rolls, cheese or liver paste or sliced sausage, and plenty of hot coffee. They gave me a key so that I could come in and go out at any hour. Even when I came back very late she made sure I had something hot to drink before I went to bed. Mr. Wegerhof worked irregular shifts at the mine, but when he was free of an evening and I was home, we would sit chatting together about everything. He was a keen football fan and his other interest was his garden. During the summer you had only to look out of the kitchen window and, whenever he was at home, there he was among the vegetables and flowers.

It was on just such a day, while I was out there talking with him and he was digging away, that he decided to go to Caux. For both him and his wife it was the greatest experience of their lives. On his return they kept telling everyone about it.

Mr. Wegerhof was on regular shift now, so was more often home in the evenings. We would sit talking in a corner of the living-room where there were two comfortable easy chairs, and as often as not, Mrs. Wegerhof would be there too, mending socks or clothes or glancing through the latest magazines. I can picture it all—the tall lamp behind us shedding its circle of light and the red-tiled stove by the wall, throwing out a comfortable warmth.

Now and then Robert would join us. He was rather thin after

all he had been through. He didn't say much, but he listened. I wondered what was going on in his mind. He gave nothing away.

Meantime news had reached the Party that Mr. Wegerhof had been to Caux and Party members would come round to try and get him to break off contact with Moral Re-Armament. This he refused to do, saying that he had in no way given up the task he had taken on when he became a revolutionary, but that he had found a better way of doing things. Finally at an official meeting he was expelled from the Party, Robert voting with the majority for his father's expulsion, as he told me later, on the grounds that it was necessary to prevent the spread of ideological confusion within the Party.

At that point we were joined in the Ruhr by a Swiss professor who had been Rector of Zürich University. The miners wanted him to give a lecture on 'The Basic Forces in European History', and this was to take place in the reception room in Gelsenkirchen at the centre that had been provided for the MRA work by the Gelsenkirchen Coal Company. We told Robert about this and invited him to come, but he would not commit himself. So Mr. Wegerhof and I went along by ourselves.

The room was absolutely crowded. The men from Moers were there. So were our friends from Essen and miners from every corner of the Ruhr. Then, just as the professor was about to begin, the door was opened carefully and in slipped Robert.

The lecture was, in the miners' words, 'etwas grundsetzliches' (very fundamental) and they listened to it intently. In the discussion afterwards they asked the most penetrating questions. Suddenly to our amazement Robert stood up and asked if he could say a few words. 'This is the second occasion on which I have heard MRA mentioned,' he said. 'The first occasion was in Stalino in Russia. There we were given eight hours of lectures on MRA. It was said there that MRA had begun well but had got off the track. But my impression now is that it is Marxism that has got off the track.'

As he gave his convictions it made a deep impression on everyone and I determined that when we got back to the Wegerhof home I would ask him for all the details. In the course of subsequent conversations with Robert, I began to get a graphic picture of the ideological battle.

Because his family was so poor he had gone into the mines at the age of fourteen. When the war came, miners were not as a rule called up, but, probably because his father was a Communist, he was drafted into the army in 1942 and sent to the Russian front. Wounded five times in the next three years, he was taken prisoner in Czechoslovakia at the capitulation and sent to Russia. His family thought he was dead, as they got no news of him for months.

In Russia, however, with his Communist background and because his father, when he heard of Robert's capture, wrote to the Party headquarters in Moscow on his behalf, he was allowed a certain freedom of movement—though not to leave Russia. He was also allowed to go to various Communist training schools to study Marxism. He finally wound up at Stalino, a big industrial town in the Donetz basin, which he said was very like the Ruhr—nothing but derricks, tall chimneys, black smoke and factory whistles.

The Stalino training school was a special one. It was not easy to get into. Every applicant was carefully investigated. It was necessary to be able to show a record of anti-fascist activity and also to have a genuine working-class background. Only men who were absolutely reliable were wanted for training at Stalino. So Robert was very proud when he and thirty other German prisoners were admitted to Stalino. Like his father he believed that Communism offered the only way to avoid repeating the mistakes of the past.

I asked him what sort of training he had been given at Stalino and how Moral Re-Armament came into it.

'The training we got fell into four principal subjects,' he said. 'Firstly, there was historical and dialectical materialism. Secondly we got the history of the Communist Party of the USSR. Thirdly we had the political and economic structure of the USSR, and fourthly the lives of Marx, Engels, Lenin and Stalin. Our professors were Germans, but the courses were supplemented by conferences with Party leaders and with Soviet authorities.

'One of the subjects that came up frequently in our discussions was how to bring the change in individuals which would lead one day to the establishing of the true Communist society. None of us had any answer to this problem. None of the Christians we had seen had been able to convince us of the possibility of a change in the way people lived.

'Then, in the middle of a course on ideological forces which could sow confusion among Communists, we were warned against Moral Re-Armament. It was the first time I had ever heard of it. Our professors described it as a Christian movement whose members had all the same faults as the rest of Christians. We were advised never to enter into contact with the Moral Re-Armament people. I thought this was a little strange, since this advice was never applied to Christians in general.'

He went on to tell me about some of the things that had struck him on his return from Stalino after five years' separation from the family. The thing he could not get away from was how different his father was. Right from the moment they met at the Bochum railway station and his father was so moved to see him again, Robert felt that a lot of things had happened which he could not explain. Then he found a Norwegian living in his room and seemingly very much a part of the family. Another point was that, at home, his father, who had formerly been pretty much of a dictator and expected instant and unquestioning obedience, was now seeking the advice of all the family on their common decisions. He had noticed, too, that when Party members came to argue, his father only told them quietly of the new things he had found. He knew that Moral Re-Armament was at the root of it but could not believe this was the thing they had been warned against in Stalino. He knew his father's background as a veteran of the class struggle, and, in spite of himself, he was impressed.

'Then father and you invited me to come and hear a Swiss professor,' he said. 'I did not intend to come but something, I don't know what, made me change my mind. The lecture, with its penetrating, ideological world view, reminded me vividly of the discussions on Moral Re-Armament we had had in Stalino. What I had been looking for suddenly became clear and I felt I just had to get up and speak. I suppose it is really because of the change in my father and of the new friends he has found.'

Two days later Robert got a bitter blow. The Party came to hear that he had attended an MRA lecture and had spoken at it, and they expelled him in turn, in spite of his still feeling completely devoted to the class struggle. His old friends, men with whom he had been fighting, often at considerable sacrifice, for a new social order, turned against him.

Then there came what he himself describes as a turning point in his life. He met a young French Jew.

This Frenchman, an ordinary worker, had for some time been with us in the Ruhr helping to put on the MRA plays throughout the Ruhr cities. Seventeen of his family had perished in German concentration camps.

'I prepared myself to listen to a long list of accusations against my nation,' Robert said. 'Nothing like that happened. This Frenchman spoke only of his own faults and the faults of his nation. His one desire was to restore for the past. In spite of the horrors he had witnessed, he had asked God to enable him to love the German people, knowing that hatred can never bring healing and reconciliation. "In order to help others," he told me, "one needs first to begin by recognising one's own wrong doings, even if they may seem very small."

'My French friend, Max,' Robert went on, 'was a man like myself, with the same faults and the same weaknesses. We had many points in common. I could see that he had found a force in his life that was able to overcome hatreds which seemed totally insurmountable. In our Marxist schools in Russia no one had told us about this new element, this factor of a transformation of society through a change in men which I could now see happening before my eyes. Suddenly the limitations of a purely materialistic ideology, unable to cure selfishness and hate, became clear to me. So I decided to follow the example of my French friend. I decided to listen for guidance and to be absolutely honest with everyone around me. Then I realised that the force which had changed my father, that we had heard about in Stalino, and that this young Frenchman personified—that force could bring the answer to the agony of our age.

'I often wondered why they gave us those lectures on MRA in Stalino. Looking back I can see now that it was at that very time Moral Re-Armament had launched its first big ideological offensive in the Ruhr. No doubt Moscow was worried by the fact that revolutionaries of long standing, the survivors of Hitler's concentration camps, had committed themselves to follow an ideology greater than Communism.'

II

The Fight For Men

NEWS of this 'greater revolution' spread like wild-fire. The ideas and the way of life embodied in the men from Moers and Essen gradually spread to other parts of the Ruhr. Active Party functionaries, men with up to thirty years' training and experience in revolutionary tactics and strategy, went to the World Assembly in Caux in spite of prohibitions and threats from the Party leadership. They came singly or as members of delegations. For all of them the common factor was that of wanting to make up their own minds as to what Moral Re-Armament really was.

They were expelled from the Party just as Bladeck, Kurowski, Stoffmehl and Heske had been. It made no difference whether they were men who had founded and led the Party in their city or whether they were just ordinary Party members—they were all expelled on the sole ground that they had been to Caux. What happened in Moers and Essen was now repeated in the industrial cities of Dortmund, Bochum, Gelsenkirchen, Gladbeck, Castrop-Rauxel and Lünen.

Whether they wanted to or not, this avant-garde of radical workers found themselves in the firing line of the ideological battle in the Ruhr. A continual warfare went on, mostly beneath the surface but flaming up powerfully during the elections for the works committee men in this centre of industry which is the biggest in Europe.

'The elections for the works committees in heavy industry are immensely important,' Max Bladeck said to us one day. 'They are actually more important than political elections. The Communists are clear about this and therefore they are doing everything in their power to win control in the factories and mines.'

This agrees exactly with what the English Communist leader, Harry Pollitt, said after the defeat of his Party in the 1950 Parliamentary elections: 'The big problems are not decided in this reactionary Parliament but through the fight for the masses in the factories and in the streets.'

In the works committee elections in 1949 and 1950 the Communists suffered a marked setback. This came out at the Party congress in Weimar on March 30th 1951.[1] Walther Ulbricht, general secretary of the 'Socialist Unity Party' and the 'strong man' in the Russian-occupied zone of Germany, was the honoured guest at this congress. After he had listened to the chairman (Max Reimann) and vice-chairman (Heinz Renner) of the German Communist Party, Ulbricht made a speech strongly criticising the Party Congress's weak points.

'The speech of our friend Renner,' he said, 'has not exactly delighted us. Why not? It may be that Members of Parliament have an awful lot to do.[2] (*Laughter.*) But when they are not there when there are works committee elections in the Ruhr in the mining industry, that is bad. (*Applause and shouts of 'Bravo!'*)

'I have been asked—"How do you like the preparations for the Party Congress?" I will tell you quite frankly. The preparations for the Party Congress showed a certain fear of criticism and self-criticism. (*Applause.*) That is your chief weakness. That's why some things which were not said before the Party Congress must be said a bit more clearly after the Party Congress. Such happenings as have been related here, that our Party has suffered such a setback in the works committee elections in the mining industry in the Gelsenkirchen area, should, before the Party

[1] The West German Communist Party had intended to hold this conference in Munich, but for some reason it was transferred to Weimar in the Soviet-occupied zone.

[2] Renner and Reimann were at that time Communist Members of Parliament in Bonn.

Congress in the Ruhr, have been made the central point of the open discussions in preparation for the Party Congress. For that is the fundamental question.

'What is reflected by the fact of this setback in Gelsenkirchen?' Although Ulbricht raised this question, in the rest of his speech he failed to give the real answer.

Following this, the works committee elections of November 1951 in the Ruhr were marked by intense activity. Within a ten-day period the Communist newspaper 'Neue Volkszeitung' printed six articles violently attacking Moral Re-Armament. The main theme through them all was, 'Don't elect the men from Caux!! Don't vote for these morally disarmed cowards—they are the enemies of the working class!' Heinz Renner, the Communist Party's vice-chairman, said warningly to Herman Stoffmehl, 'We are determined to destroy Moral Re-Armament's power in the works committees and thereby reduce it to a sect and nothing else.'

Every day the Communists had their people stationed at the entrances to the pits giving out leaflets, and every day there were new rumours spread through open and underground whispering campaigns. High-ranking Party functionaries were active everywhere. One such was Willy Agatz, one of the ablest trade union men the Communists had in the Ruhr. From 1946 to 1947 he was vice-chairman of the West German Miners Union with some 500,000 members. In 1949 he was elected to the West German Parliament and although from then on he had to work from Bonn, he still regarded it as his chief work to back up the Ruhr miners in the fight to get their Party comrades successfully elected to the pit committees.

On the 2nd of November Willy Agatz was the chief speaker at a miners' conference the Communists held in Bochum. Next day he wrote in 'Neue Volkszeitung': 'In the works committee elections this year it is our task to carry on the battle against Moral Re-Armament's agents among the workers with the greatest energy.'

On the 4th of November he addressed the Communist works committee members of the Essen and Gelsenkirchen districts. His cry was—'Build up active cells in the pits!' Ostensibly these cells were to work against military re-armament, fight for world peace, and support the workers' demands. But their real aim was to win back the power the Communists had lost in the mining industry in 1949–50.

Nor was it only Willy Agatz who left his work in Bonn to come to the mines of the Ruhr. His Party comrades, Max Reimann and Heinz Renner, got to work too.

Just as these men visited their people in the evenings, we were out meeting the men who had decided to stand for 'what is right' for the individual worker and for the mines as a whole. After we had spent an evening with one of the works committee men, it might happen that the next day he would be visited by men from the Russian-occupied zone. They would try to talk him into working for the Party or invite him to the East zone. They would tell him that there he could study the Peoples' factories and see what advantages the workers had achieved. The next evening it would be our turn to advance again.

'Our Party has suffered a serious setback in the works committee elections in the Gelsenkirchen area,' Walther Ulbricht had said at the Party congress in Weimar. And he had asked, 'What is reflected by the fact of this setback?'

What Walther Ulbricht did not say was that the key men in seven of the biggest pits in the Gelsenkirchen area had been to Caux and had been expelled from the Party.

What happened to these men in the elections of November 1951?

The committee chairman in the Bergmannsglück Pit (which employs 3,600 men) had been an active Party functionary for twenty-eight years. After he had got to know the ideology of Moral Re-Armament, the Party did everything it could to get him out of the works committee. Before the elections they attacked him by agitating in the pit and through the press.

'Neue Volkszeitung' published three articles defaming him. He was re-elected committee chairman.

Another miner who was a member of the works committee at the Bonifacius Pit (3,000 men) and who had also been in Caux, said to us, 'I have no chance of being elected this time.' However he got 208 votes more than in the previous election. His closest Party friend in the committee was one of the founders of the Communist Party in Gelsenkirchen. He, too, had been in Caux that autumn and he, too, was re-elected with an increased vote. The committee chairman in the same pit came out top of the list with the most votes of anyone, and so continued in his job. He had been in Caux for the second time.

On the evening before the election in the Graf Moltke Pit (3,500 men) the Communists put out leaflets violently attacking the committee chairman, who had consistently gone in for Moral Re-Armament's ideas, and a Communist who that summer had been expelled from the Party because he had been to Caux. The attack was so timed that they had no chance of putting their side of the matter before the workers. They were both re-elected, together with four other committee members who had all been to Caux that year. The committee chairman was elected for the third time to represent all 25,000 workers of the coal company.

In the Zollverein 3/10 Pit Fritz Heske was re-elected and continued as committee chairman.

In the big Gelsenkirchen area there was one pit where the Communists made progress, the Nordstern mine. There they won eleven out of the thirteen workers' seats on the committee.

In the Western section, Max Bladeck got more votes than in the previous election and continued as committee chairman in the Rheinpreussen IV Pit in Moers.

In the Northern section of the Ruhr, in Castrop-Rauxel, there is the Erin Pit (4,500 men). Both the chairman and the vice-chairman of the committee (and both had previously been

Communists) were attacked because of what they had done for Moral Re-Armament, but both were re-elected with 200 more votes than in the previous election. Two further committee members, who had been in Caux just before the elections, also got more votes than they had ever had before.

Farther to the north, where the seams lie deeper and deeper under the earth, there is the Victoria Pit (3,400 men) in Lünen. The leading Communist on the committee, who was at the same time chairman of the Party in Lünen-Süd, had also been in Caux that year. On his return he had been expelled from the Party and had also been the victim of violent slanders. One day he was attacked in the street and knocked down. This made his closest friend in the Party, who was also on the works committee, rally solidly to his support and leave the Party. Fourteen others left the Party for the same reason. In the elections he got 189 votes more than in the previous elections. His comrade on the committee, who had stuck by him, got more votes than anyone else in the pit.

In view of 1951's increased voting, the impression of the two previous years was strengthened, namely, that the Communists were receiving a marked setback in the works committees.

This was confirmed by Hubert Stein, a member of the central executive of the West German Miners' Union. At a World Conference in 1951 he said, 'During the last three years the Communist vote in the works committees of the Ruhr mining industry has gone down from 72 per cent to 25 per cent and that is chiefly due to Moral Re-Armament.'

Was it a political battle we were waging?

Those of us who were in the thick of the fight knew that that was not the case. What we were living for was something that went far deeper than any political programme.

In sharing the cares and joys, the ups and downs of our friends, we ourselves became a part of the life that was stirring in the Ruhr.

I know no other place where I have seen the working man's

wife exert herself so hard—and mean so much—as in this industrial community. She is up between four and five in the morning, prepares a meal and gets her man off to work. Then there are the children to look after, the house to clean, the washing to do. There is dinner to get, and supper, and there are always clothes to mend and get ready right on till late at night. She is the last to go to bed. She goes about her daily duties gladly and she has a heart so big that she can make the sourest pessimist crack a smile. There is something regal about these Ruhr mothers, large and solid, as they like to be. And what they can do when they set their minds to it! Not infrequently mother is the boss in the home.

On the rare occasions when she finds time, she goes with neighbouring wives to the 'fashion show' at one of the big stores. There she likes to sit over a cup of coffee and a couple of pieces of rich cake with an extra portion of whipped cream on top. They gossip and laugh and enjoy themselves—and discuss the latest fashion in dresses and corsets. When they go home they may or may not have bought clothing, but they will certainly have popped into the food department and invested in a big German sandwich sausage or two and some meat—things that are always good to have in the house.

Her husband, the Ruhr working man, looks upon it as his honour to turn out quality work. He actually enjoys his work. There is no cutting of corners here, whether at the work bench, the coal face or the foundry floor. Many a time have I stopped to wonder at their skill and precision. It almost seems as if they have an intuitive understanding of the material they are working with. And they have a quality in their lives too. One sees it right away—in the home, in the kitchen, or in the relationship to the children. When the workers go to the theatre or to the concert hall they choose the best—Goethe, Schiller, Beethoven. They go with such a mixture of expectation, respect and humility that the evening is an experience. The annual summer performances of classical drama are attended by the workers in their hundreds of thousands.

Of course there are those who prefer the public house. There the discussion waxes hot over wages, piece-work rates, over Schalke or Borussia (the two top ranking German football teams), or over the many burning questions of current political affairs. As the evening wears on the voices rise more and more, while those not taking part in the discussion just sit drinking, staring vacantly into space.

Sundays have a charm of their own. That is the day whole families go out together. All over the Ruhr you meet them out walking in the country, in the deer parks, visiting the exhibitions and displays. They can spend hours over flowers or watching the birds, or poring over technical displays and machinery. They have an incredible knack for detail. Others sit by the banks of the canals watching the boats and barges and all the life of the river. Or they find a good level spot by the autobahn where they can sit and watch the cars whizzing by. But the high point of the day is when father buys dinner for the whole family, an ample meal in a restaurant seething with people, but where you can sit on as long as you want while the orchestra plays all the known and loved tunes.

They are violent in their feelings and reactions, dynamic like the Ruhr itself. They possess a force and energy that seems about to explode at any moment unless harnessed and heightened to serve some great purpose.

One evening when we were sitting talking in the home of one of the works committee chairmen, he and his wife told us how they had just been literally at blows with one another. 'I got home a little late from work,' he told us, 'and then she began scolding and saying that I had been having a dram or two again. "How dare you say a thing like that?" I said. One word led to another till finally I snatched up the dish of meat from the table and hurled it against the wall and the gravy splashed all over the carpet.'

At this point his wife took up the tale, 'Then I rushed into the bedroom and slammed the door. "You can clean it up yourself, you swine!" I shouted.'

Her husband went on, 'After my outburst I began to think and in the silence it came clearly to me—It was my fault. Ask her forgiveness.'

With freedom and laughter they were able to tell us the whole story and how they had now found a stronger unity.

We became a part of these people's daily lives. But it was something deeper than the trivial round of everyday life that made us become more than just good friends.

It was not uncommon for these workers' families in the Ruhr to have close relatives in the Russian-occupied zone—a brother or sister, an uncle or cousin, or sometimes parents. It might happen that one day they would get a visit from a Party agent from the East zone. He would converse at length and show an interest in all the family's doings. He was a man who knew how to play his cards. As he was bidding them a friendly farewell, out would come his trump card, 'If you don't support us you never know what might happen to your parents!'

I know one family where the husband, after a quarter of a century's loyal work for the Party, was expelled because he went to Caux. One day a couple of Party functionaries came to his wife, who was still a Party member, demanding that she divorce him on ideological grounds. For her the question became a simple moral problem. She decided to stick with her husband.

There were two brothers who hated each other. Dieter was a fiery Communist. Klaus identified himself with Moral Re-Armament's ideas. One day they met in the street and Dieter made some slighting remarks. It came to blows and both had to stay home from work the next day. That gave Klaus time to look into his own heart and he began to see his relation to his brother in a new light. He saw that for years he had been jealous of Dieter and been bitter because Dieter had taken first place. It was no longer a question of combating his brother's ideology, but of whether he had the courage to go to his brother and ask his forgiveness for the bitterness and hatred that had divided them.

Another of our friends was Arno. He had been active in the Communist movement from 1922 on and, among other things, had been a founder of the Party in one of the mining towns. When the Moral Re-Armament play was in the Ruhr in 1949 and 1950, he was a bitter opponent. His wife became interested, however, and saw 'The Forgotten Factor'. Over a period of two years he gradually came to the personal conviction that this new ideology was the right one. No one could shake this conviction although, in his own living, he had not yet fully faced the consequences of it. His big problem was alcohol and his former friends knew how to make use of his weakness. But gradually Arno found the faith and inner power strong enough to overcome this constant temptation and all that went with it. On one big family occasion he and his wife had decided to receive the Church's blessing as an expression of their commitment to the faith they had found. The evening before, a number of their old friends gathered in their home. Among them was a Party comrade who had been quite a long time in the Russian-occupied zone. This man tried the whole time to get Arno to take a dram 'for old friendship's sake', but finally he had to give up. He was the last to leave the house, about 3 o'clock in the morning, and as he went he said, 'Arno, I hate what you stand for, but I respect your decision.'

There were men who were enticed with tempting jobs and promises of money. There were others who were threatened with physical ill-treatment unless they were willing to do what the Party demanded of them.

These things went on all the time. This situation reached deep into these men's lives and raised simple moral problems. Our only task was to help these different individuals to solve these problems.

How were we to help? We could not prescribe for them what

they should do. We could not regulate or direct them or screw them up morally. They had to solve the conflict themselves, from the inside. They had themselves to discover what was right and go by that.

How helpless, ill prepared and unworthy I felt often in the face of such deep human problems! I well knew the same battle going on inside myself. I and my friends knew from experience what the forces were which warred in our own natures. That was why we were so much at one with these men and women.

One day I was invited to meet some tough, well-trained revolutionaries. But when I heard who was coming, among them a Communist whom I could not stand, I lost all desire to go. 'No, I won't meet that man!' However, clarity came through a quiet time. 'You have been dominated by his strong personality and far-reaching opinions. You are just looking for an escape. But you don't need to be guided any longer by fear or inferiority feelings. Just be yourself. Go and fight for what you know is right.' At the same time I knew I could neither do this by my own efforts nor act a part. A new freedom and caring needed to be born in me—a need I knew only God could satisfy. I cannot explain what happened, but it is a fact that during the evening I told this man all about it and was able to laugh over my having been afraid of him. I was able to talk freely about the convictions I had come to and for the first time we became real friends—individuals who knew our need of one another in spite of differences in our ways of thinking.

On another occasion I suddenly noticed that I no longer liked my friend Jens. We had worked together for years and had had many a friendly set-to. But this time it was as if there was a wall of ice between us. We were 'united' yet divided. Something had fallen apart and I could not get it put together again. Then I decided to be absolutely honest about my motives. Again the inner voice spoke with freeing clarity. I had actually become crusted with jealousy. A group of our German friends were to go to a conference and Jens had been invited to go with them. I had not been invited. Thoughts began to go on inside me—'I am really better fitted for this task'—and my brain mobilised countless arguments in my own favour. I had actually wanted Jens to be eliminated in one way or another so that I could go instead. That was what my real motives were. That was what I was like. The moment I realised the naked truth about myself, I experienced afresh the power that had carried me through the dark days at Møller Street 19—Christ's forgiveness, Christ's love. Without a trace of bitterness I was able to say to myself, 'Jens is the right one!' As we talked without beating about the bush or making excuses, the wall of ice melted. A new unity was forged between us.

These simple points which I have experienced time after time and which I have seen happening in the lives of others also, have shown me that I, and everyone who is willing to pay the price, can find a freedom day by day that no individual, no collective, no power system can take from us. That brings me back to the question I raised earlier—Was it a political battle we were waging?

It was much more than that. It was a battle to set men free, a battle to find out the reasons for our hate and jealousy, the reasons why we are at the mercy of our desires, why we allow ourselves to be used by evil forces to divide men and divide the society we live in. It was a battle to stick to and follow the truth that the inner voice was revealing to us, and to accept the power that can do in people what they cannot do for themselves.

That was the daily battle we were waging. We were facing mighty forces, facing men with an impressive capacity for sacrificing time, money, energy, personal feelings and their own comfort. They were strong—and ruthless. Since they believed that the end justifies the means, they thought nothing of exploiting all the weaknesses and wrong tendencies in human nature. Since they worked on the assumption that you can't change human nature, they used everything to win control and keep it. If man cannot be changed he must needs be exploited to further the aims of revolution. What happens to the individual means nothing.

On our side, however, we went on the experience that human nature can be changed through the power of God. The whole battle was a battle in and for men, not to exploit them but to change and inspire them.

We had to learn that the total and ruthless enlistment of certain people in order to secure domination over others could only be overcome when we were borne up by a power greater than ourselves and our political ideas and systems. We were facing men who represented a world force, a militant ideology that was not halted by frontiers but stretched from the Ruhr on through East Berlin to Moscow and Peking. If we were to be able to meet the deep personal needs in such men, needs that are decisive for a man's life, it would take more than the will to sacrifice, the high ideals and convictions that we ourselves could provide. It would take divine guidance and inspiration. It would take the power which can create a new type of man, make man the person he was meant to be, made as he was 'in the image of God'.

This is what had begun to happen in people like Max and Paul and Fritz and their families. They had a new glint in their eyes, a stronger fire in their conviction, and a new love which overcame all attacks directed against them. Indeed it was they who were on the offensive, waging a battle from morning to night to win their bitter opponents. For Max and Paul and Fritz and the others knew from their own experience that the men and women who were doing everything to crush them were caught in their own toils—without knowing it. An ideology based on using and exploiting people, carries no guarantee for any individual. No one can feel safe. Just as they exploit others so they let themselves in for being exploited in turn. For them, as for all of us, there is only one road to freedom—to find a higher power, to move on to an ideology that does not just bind but which frees and inspires.

That was what they had found, Max and Paul and Fritz and the others. That was what amazed and attracted their Party comrades and compelled them to admit that these men had found a freedom and a power greater than anything they had yet seen anywhere else. They had to admit that Max and the others were now thinking in a way which went far beyond them.

The main thing we had to do, therefore, was to stand united in this vital and exciting task, one that demanded more than our human capabilities. We had to stand there in the midst of the situation just as it was, helpless and with empty hands, yet with hope and faith and the certainty that when man listens, God speaks, and when men obey, God acts.

12

The Nordstern Mine

ONE of the places in the Ruhr which always has a kind of fascination for me is the Nordstern–Gelsenberg complex of pits and chemical plants in Gelsenkirchen–Horst. Many a time as I have been driving past I have had to stop on the bridge over the Emscher–Rhine canal and watch the tankers and heavy barges floating gently and peacefully down stream. Along the banks of the canal, boys sit holding long fishing poles waiting for a bite. Nearby a farmer is ploughing in his field. The tanker barges draw in to the Gelsenberg Benzin (petrol) wharves, a huge chemical plant whose cooling towers, belching out clouds of grey and white vapour, dominate the view. The chimneys of the power station reach up like long fingers to the sky. The maze of pipes by the distilling tower gleam like silver in the sunshine.

Across the canal at the Nordstern mine's harbour, other barges are waiting to be loaded up with coke and coal. I might see the gas flame from the coke oven flare up, and catch the sharp, sourish smell that comes from a coke plant. Across the rise I might glimpse the new pithead gear of the Nordstern mine where, under ground, 3,000 grimy, sweaty men are hewing out the coal needed for the Gelsenberg Benzin power station, for the coke plant, and for the harbour from where the 'black gold' is exported to other parts of the world.

The three different sections of the whole complex together employ some 9,000 men.

In the Communists' battle to win the Ruhr, Nordstern was their chief stronghold. In 1946 a group of determined men had decided to get control of the mine. They were only a few, but they knew what they wanted and they carried out their plan with unwavering thoroughness and a burning will to win. They succeeded. Soon they were in complete control of the workers and were putting pressure on management. In the works committee they could do just what they wanted. Out of eleven members, ten were Communists.

Once they had achieved power in Nordstern they were not slow to use it. Over and over again they passed resolutions supporting the Communist Party's work in other parts of the world, and on big occasions telegrams of greetings and congratulations went from this mine to the President of the Russian-occupied zone and to Josef Stalin in Moscow. Members of the works committee went to the East zone for training and instructions. Party comrades from the East came to Nordstern and got jobs there.

When 'The Forgotten Factor' was presented in the Hans Sachs House in Gelsenkirchen in the spring of 1950, some of us were invited to meet the works committee and the manager of the mine. Four of us went—an English miner, Geoffrey, Jens and I. When we got to the manager's office we found there only the manager himself and the one non-Communist member of the works committee. We conversed for about twenty minutes. Suddenly the door opened and in came the ten Communists in a body. They operated the whole time as a unit and at once seized the initiative. They had carefully prepared what they were going to say and who would say it. We listened. Their two most skilled debaters put forward their view, summarised the world situation, and maintained that the class war was the only way to break the capitalist system. They regarded Moral Re-Armament as a hindrance to the class war and therefore an enemy of peace.

When they came to a halt we spoke up. In the age of the atom bomb, we suggested, the logical consequence of Karl Marx's theory of class war would be total destruction. 'In such a situation, therefore, it is necessary to take stock afresh, look the realities in the face, and draw conclusions—a thing every true Marxist is always ready to do. What the world needs is a far-reaching change in people and a new thinking that creates unselfish teamwork. Here is a force which is working for that kind of change of human nature in everyone in every part of the world.'

The ten left the meeting in the same manner as they had come. None of them gave any indication of what he personally felt. We remained talking with the manager. He was keen to know more about this way of life and of the world work we were taking part in. He had been to the Hans Sachs House several times himself and had seen 'The Forgotten Factor'. He fully agreed with us that change was the only way, and that we must begin with ourselves right where we are.

Next day the 'Neue Volkszeitung' had an article on the visit to Nordstern with the headline, ' "Moralists' Threaten Trade-Union Men with the Atom Bomb".' The sub-head ran, 'Agents of USA Imperialism get the one correct answer from works committee members.'

In November 1950 a strike broke out suddenly in the mine. Two of the Communists in the works committee had been fired for provocative behaviour. Less than thirty minutes later Radio Leipzig in the Russian-occupied zone was broadcasting the news and urging all miners in the Ruhr to come out on strike in sympathy. The works committee itself sent strike committees round the Ruhr to get all the 90,000 men of the G.B.A.G. Company, of which Nordstern is a part, out on strike with them. The national executive of the German Miners Union had declared the strike illegal, but all the same the danger was imminent, as the strike was obviously ideological in character, its ultimate aim being to cripple the economic and industrial life of the Ruhr.

The strike committee's hopes were not fulfilled. After three days the Nordstern miners returned to work. The plans for sympathetic strikes came to nothing. What happened?

Some of the men who stood closest to the developments can best tell the story.

The manager of the Gelsenkirchen G.B.A.G. group of mines reported: 'There is just one reason why we were able to end the strike so quickly—the men in responsible positions had become acquainted with the principles of Moral Re-Armament. That applies equally to the employers, the trade union officials, and the central works committee of the company, irrespective of whether they were Socialists or Christian Democrats. That led to our finding a common plan which we were able to follow without any defections.'

North Rhine-Westphalia's Economic and Social Minister, Dr. Arthur Straeter, said, 'That the strike did not spread was due to the fact that responsible works committee members in different parts of the Ruhr had adopted the ideology of Caux. They averted a sympathetic strike which could have caused a very serious situation.'

Fritz Heske, chairman of the works committee at the Zollverein 3/10 pit, said, 'The illegal strike committee came to see me at Zollverein. A year earlier, as a Communist, I would have been a hundred per cent with them. This time I told them I was working on the principle of what is right. So I sent them away. In similar fashion, quite a number of the works committee were able to see through this strike committee's plan and reject it.'

Gradually the new ideas began to take root and every summer delegations from Nordstern went to the World Assemblies in Caux and in America. Men who took a clear stand for a moral ideology were the objects of constant attack but they did not let themselves be frightened off.

In the works committee elections of November 1951 the Communists were able to maintain their big majority. However, this was not because the Communists had most of the workers behind them, but because the others were split by individual ambition and jealousy. No one would withdraw in favour of another and this led to far too many candidates' names appearing on the election lists. Thereby the vote was split up and the individualists did not get enough votes to get elected.

The next elections were held in the spring of 1953. A new law had laid down that these elections should now take place every second year. In addition, the works committees had been increased by several additional members. As usual, the Communist Party sent out a flood of leaflets warning the voters against 'morally re-armed candidates'. The results of the elections were so remarkable that the Socialist daily in the Ruhr, the 'Westphalische Rundschau', used the headline—'Election Sensation'. Out of the twenty-three members on the new works committee, only three were Communists.

The man who was chairman of the works committee, both before and after this election, was a Marxist who had followed the theory of the class struggle all his life. Like many another in the Ruhr he had grown up in the Socialist youth movement and had joined the Communist Party in the 1930's. He was one of the workers who gave everything for social justice and world peace. We were often in his home. He would keep coming back to something that seemed to have made an indelible impression on him—the change he had seen in the mine manager. Here was a Marxist faced with an employer who no longer was just out for his own profit, no longer trying to force his own will on others—a man with new motives. 'We can rely on him,' he said of his boss, 'because he is frank and honest. He is actually trying to find out what is right, so we can trust him. He listens to us, so we can work together with him.'

This Marxist realised that there was an ideology above class. He discovered something new, that an employer who fights for thorough-going change of motives among his own crowd can encounter just as much opposition as a worker risks meeting from his friends when he decided to do what is morally right. He realised that a real friend is a man who can meet the deepest longings and need in another's heart, regardless of what class or race he may belong to.

One day this committee chairman became seriously ill. As he felt his life ebbing away, what he most wanted was to talk to someone about all he had on his heart. He asked for the mine manager to come and the manager was with him during his last hours.

On the 4th of June 1956, some of us were invited to a meeting in the manager's office. This time something very different happened than on that first visit Geoffrey and Jens and I had made to the Nordstern mine six years earlier.

The manager and one of the workers had had the thought that they should send greetings from the Nordstern mine to Dr. Frank Buchman by telephone for his seventy-eighth birthday, and tell him that they stood together with him in the ideological battle for the world. We sat around the big table—the manager, under-manager, treasurer, four members of the works committee, a worker from the coal face, and four of the office staff. Herman Stoffmehl, Robert Wegerhof and Willy Benedens were there too, and several others. Together they telephoned from the Ruhr to London, giving Dr. Buchman their heartiest congratulations and inviting him to visit the Ruhr again. As they spoke, with Frank Buchman in London were his German friends Max and Grethe Bladeck, Paul and Lina Kurowski and Fritz Heske.

'Hier ist die Zeche Nordstern in Gelsenkirchen,' said the manager into the phone. 'Glückauf, Frank! We are thinking back to the year 1950 when you were with us in Gelsenkirchen and when the ideological foundations for rebuilding Germany were laid in the Hans Sachs House.'

He was followed by Willy Benedens and several others.

Then Stoffmehl took the phone. 'Hello, Frank!' he said. 'I want to send you our warmest wishes, from my wife as well as myself. Both of us, and our family, have you to thank for the new life we have found. I hope you will be spared for many years so that we can fight together with you.'

But what I remember best from Nordstern was an experience that happened in the summer of 1956. Men from all sections in the mine had asked for a performance of 'The Dictator's Slippers', a play by Peter Howard. In connection with this, a Canadian friend and I had agreed to give out tickets at the mine. We set ourselves up in the hall where the wages were paid, right by the entrance to the showers, a place where all the workers came by. We were on edge to know how things would go. Some of the men were not to be played with. They were deep-rooted enemies of all we stood for. For my part, I was a little nervous to begin with. It was like going into the firing line. We had set up a table and with the tickets we had a great deal of literature. In an hour's time the tickets for both performances had gone. For the next hours we gave out literature, nearly as many pieces as there were miners at Nordstern.

In the midst of all this, one of the works committee members rang up the under-manager and demanded that we be removed. When this was turned down, he tried to enlist some of the men in the hall, sending us glances of hatred as he went around talking to them one after the other. But he had no success and finally left.

As I stood in the midst of that stream of humanity—miners on the way in to work, others on their way home—I was gripped by an amazing feeling of oneness and fellowship with these workers whose furrowed faces and bodies were marked by adversity and weariness. The fate of every single man was my fate. It was as if I could feel all that was going on in them as they streamed past us. This was a war generation who in former days had put all their trust in the Weimar Republic and had experienced disillusionment and collapse. The younger ones among them had been misled and exploited by dictatorship and now they had a look of cynicism and hopelessness in their eyes. There were men among them who had waited for years for the return of their nearest and dearest from prisoner-of-war camps. There were others who had gone through losing their closest comrades in explosions and accidents in the mines. But there was also a glimpse of something else in their eyes. As they came towards us with a hand outstretched to take one of the newspapers, as they stopped to chat for a moment, as they looked over the literature and smiled—then I saw the inner man breaking through the outer shell. These were men seeking after life, men full of songs and dreams and poetry and a deep longing for a world in which we would understand one another, in which brotherhood and peace would become realities in everyday life—in the home and in the pit galleries, between individuals and in the relations between nations.

These men—a voice inside me seemed to be saying—and, with them, all the workers of the world, were never meant to be pawns in a political system whose aim was power. Nor were they meant to be slaves in an economic system whose aim was profit. Was it not worth while devoting the rest of my life in helping to realise their true human worth, to realise their songs and dreams and longings, to liberate their energies—energies which, when set free, could lead the whole of humanity to a new era?

Can this happen? This is the question I ask myself as I think back. And suddenly I know that it can. For it has begun to happen! In my mind's eye I see a whole series of our friends who have found new life and a new idea. There is something special about these men from the Ruhr. They thought in world terms in the days when they were fighting for the Communist idea, and immediately they had won their way to something bigger they again thought in big terms, thought about Germany, Europe, the whole world. They knew that the war of ideologies must be fought and won on a world front.

I can remember mornings when they went straight from the night shift by car to the Parliament building in Bonn, had talks there until late in the evening, and then drove back to the Ruhr to go straight on to the night shift again. On these men's initiative European conferences for workers and students, journalists and leaders of industry, parliamentarians and churchmen, were held in the Ruhr. When delegations from Asia and Africa came to Germany on the way to Caux or on the way home, the workers would invite them to the Ruhr to tell them of the ideological battle they themselves were waging there and about the new spirit which had been created in the mines through the changing of men.

They themselves travelled too. I remember how August Metzing and Johan Holzhäuser went to Italy to meet the workers in the Montecatini factories and in the Falck steel works. Fritz Heske talked to the miners in Kiruna in North Sweden. Paul Kurowski talked to factory workers in the 'red belt' of Paris and to dockers in London and Rotterdam. Bladeck and Kurowski spent months in different parts of India and Africa. Bladeck made a trip to the Far East and in Japan he played a part in the uniting of the Socialist Party which at that time had been split into two warring factions. Wegerhof got six months' leave without pay to visit the miners and workers all over India. Max and Paul and their friends from Essen and Moers went to Washington and, at a time when the waves of anti-Communism were high in America, they gave politicians and Congressmen a powerful challenge, namely that the decisive question is not how to combat Communism but how to create a superior ideology and make it effective! They gave the Wall Street bankers an inspiring glimpse of what financial men could do if they let the needs of the whole world be the determining factor in their thinking.

Their wives played an equally important part. In July 1955, speaking in Caux, Lina Kurowski said, 'Two years ago I was with a team in India. Last year I was with a team in Africa. And Paul and I have been in Australia and many other countries. Everywhere the problems are the same and they must be solved inside families.

'My husband, who was for twenty-six years in the Communist Party, was responsible for the training of Party members and the young people. But he didn't train me. There was war between us. I knew there was hate in his heart, hate born out of the days of misery and need we have been through. But I had no ideology—only a wish not to change before he did. I was waiting for him to change and prove he meant it. But when that happened, a great change took place in me too. It was through Moral Re-Armament that we really found one another.

'That is why I stand beside my husband in this fight. If we women would fight more in peacetime, our men would not have to shed their blood in wartime.' [1]

I could see them before me as they stood shoulder to shoulder with the steel workers of France, the dockers in England, the factory workers of Italy, the miners in North Sweden, the aeroplane mechanics in America, trade-union men in India and Japan. They came from Germany, and they came to restore for what Germany had done wrong in the past. Without political or diplomatic machinery they created unity and reconciliation. Peace—they said—is not just an idea. Peace is people becoming different.

My thoughts, which had been following them all around the world, came back to the Ruhr with hope and gratitude—the Ruhr with its mines and factories, with its smoke and dirt, with its flower-decked parks and green open spaces, and with its people—men of deep feelings and strong wills.

[1] On the 15th November 1958, on Mackinac Island, Michigan, Lina Kurowski died after a three months' illness. She was fifty-eight. She and Paul had been there fighting for people all summer at the MRA World Assembly in America.

13

'Berlin Depends On You'

In the same way as the Ruhr became a real home and a part of my life, so did Berlin—that vast, uneasy city marooned 160 miles from West Germany, entirely surrounded by the Soviet-occupied zone. I was in Berlin for more than a year altogether, though I made various trips to the 'West' at different times in between. My first visit to Berlin, incidentally, which I made by plane from Hanover along the air corridor to the Tempelhof airport, was to join the Norwegian professor I had met first in Grini. He was in Berlin for a week as the first guest lecturer from Norway at the Free University, in the autumn of 1951.

It is difficult to describe Berlin. It is something special. It is the people, the atmosphere, the very air—everything. It has to be experienced. It is the solid, two-decker buses where the conductor invariably talks away to himself, cracks jokes, and seems to be thoroughly enjoying life. It is the characteristic landmark of the ruined Gedächtniskirche. It is the Kurfurstendamm, formerly the centre of the very wealthy, a mixture of Karl Johan (Oslo's main street), Piccadilly, and Broadway all rolled into one. It is the cafés, the restaurants, the new cinemas and department stores with their huge display windows. It is a city of taste and artistic feeling, of quality and novel ideas. The night life, the crowds walking around, the neon signs, the illuminations, all remind one of Paris or London or New York.

It is the Schillertheater, risen anew out of the ruins all around and everything that a theatre should be in appearance, acoustics and equipment, down to the last detail. Berliners love the drama, art and music. As well as the plays of Shakespeare, Goethe,

Schiller, Hauptmann, Molière, you will often find the theatres giving Ibsen and Strindberg. The Berlin Philharmonic is a favourite with everybody. Every year there are international festival weeks with concerts by the best-known orchestras, opera, ballet, plays and films from all over the world. Amazingly the former capital of the German Reich, in spite of its present situation, has become a centre of culture, of international conferences, of industrial and agricultural exhibitions. For this, huge and beautifully planned exhibition grounds have been laid out in the area round the Funkturm, the tall radio tower with its restaurant on top.

Berlin is also Grunewald, that great open park area with its wonderful woods and the many lakes—Wannsee, Hafel, Teglersee, Nikolasee. For the average Berliner these have taken the place of the North Sea coast or the southern mountains to which in pre-war days he used to go. Grunewald's few square miles are now the 'lungs' of the city, as well as providing rest and relaxation for nerves that are constantly under pressure from so many sides.

Where Grunewald begins, just on the borders of the exhibition grounds by the Funkturm, there is a fair-sized hill, covered with green in summer and covered with children coming down the slopes on skis in winter. The hill provides the only ski jump within the city. Underneath, however, it is no real hill of earth and rock, but a vast pile of stones and bricks and rubble heaped together there when the ruins of the centre of the city were laboriously cleared away. The war destroyed most of the city. Seventy-five million cubic metres of rubble were left strewn in its wake. It has taken ten years to clear it up and there is still much to be done. It seemed an absolutely hopeless job at the outset, but thousands of Berliners started in to do it with nothing but their bare hands. One of the things that struck me most on that first visit to Berlin was to see the women, old and young, some indeed obviously over sixty, dressed in trousers and pullovers and with scarves wound round their heads, working away in spite of the cold, in spite of the shortage of food, to clear away the broken bricks and rubbish.

Berlin is also the City of Refugees—a constant stream, over 1,000 every week, month after month, year after year. Always there is a crowd of them, escaped from the East, exhausted, expectant, waiting in the Kuno Fischerstrasse to be screened. Whole families, carrying all they now possess in a few untidy bundles, wait patiently at Tempelhof for the chance of an air trip out to West Germany. One day in the Neu Kladow refugee camp (in Berlin), where a large percentage are youngsters of the Soviet-occupied zone's 'People's Police', I was much moved when a young refugee with whom I had been talking insisted that I accept a wrought-iron candlestick he had made, in token of friendship. To this unceasing stream of humanity, Berlin represents the door to freedom. Here they hope to find a new purpose in life.

In the midst of this atmosphere of unconquerable spirit, of ruins, of rebuilding, of prolific cultural life, the Berliner lives. He likes to study life sitting in one of the many cafés that border the Kurfurstendamm, sipping his coffee accompanied by a piece of his favourite cake. Or he scrapes his pfennigs together and takes the bus out to Wannsee, where he can swim and stretch out in the sun and have a good time. There are two and a half million people in West Berlin and I can remember days at Wannsee when the beach was so crowded that it was almost impossible to find a place to sit down. Berliners have the art of being able to make the most of whatever situation they may find themselves in. Their motto might almost be: 'Enjoy yourself. It's later than you think.' Years of political tension have created in them a need to relax, and they enjoy such moments all the more because deep down in their hearts they know that there is no escape from the realities of the situation. They feel deeply that the freedom they still possess depends upon them, on each one of these two and a half million ordinary men and women, and on how they meet the challenge that faces them daily.

All the above refers, of course, to West Berlin. In East Berlin the picture is very different. The reader will understand if in this chapter I deliberately avoid mentioning many definite names.

I

I will never forget one evening in the home of a leading trade-unionist, the first Berlin home in which I stayed. We were celebrating the birthday of my hostess. The family were there and several friends. I sat beside an old lady of over seventy. She was friendly but a little aloof, and at first we talked only of the weather and other general topics. Then I happened to ask her about Berlin as it was in her younger days. At once her eyes lit up as she began to give me a lively and interesting description of the great past of this city. It had been wonderful in the days of the Kaiser, she recalled. There had been years of undisturbed peace under Wilhelm the Second, and with his sure hand on the helm, life in Berlin had been full. I could almost picture it as she spoke—the Tiergarten with its well-kept, green, tree-shaded lawns where Berliners loved to walk in the freshness of the morning hours; the open-air cafés where one could bring one's own sandwiches and order delicious coffee. If you were lucky you might even see the Kaiser himself ride by, a bit on the stout side perhaps, but radiating confidence and friendliness, nodding to everyone he met. Then there was Unter den Linden on a May evening, with its famous lime trees and festive lighting; and the music—Linke, Strauss, Lehar, whose care-free, joyous strains were symbols of hope and happiness. Ah, those were the days, truly a wonderful time!

We were interrupted by our hostess pressing us to have another cup of coffee and one more piece of her apple pastry. The old lady fell silent, dreaming still of those bygone days. They were gone for ever. One glance out of the window revealed how different the present was—a bombed and gutted house with only gaping holes for windows, roofless, open to the sky. The German Empire had vanished with the Treaty of Versailles. All that was left of Hitler's vaunted Third Reich was this mass of ruins. They stood there, the ruins, like a judgment and a gravestone. And today? Today there was fear in men's minds, fear of the future, fear undefined but ever present. Unter den Linden that had once echoed to the strains of 'The Merry Widow', now stood silent and deserted. From the Brandenburger Tor to where the Kaiser's palace used to stand, the eye was arrested by block after block of buildings displaying propaganda slogans and enormous pictures of Marx, Lenin and Stalin, proclaiming a new era in the history of man.

Our host, Georg, sat at the other end of the table. He reminded me a great deal of Max Bladeck. Grey-haired, not very tall, he was a dynamic, revolutionary character, a clear thinker and clever strategist, equally at home at the chess board as in the political and trade-union field. As a young man he had been an active member of the Spartacus group supporting Rosa Luxemburg and Karl Liebknecht, but after the notorious Moscow trials he had broken with the Communist Party. He had overheard our conversation, so later in the evening he told me more about his city—the bitter war years, the terrible days of fighting in 1945, and the decisive first post-war months. It was a fascinating story of the Berliners' fight for freedom, one I had never heard before, so I made copious notes as we sat talking far into the night after the other guests had gone.

In November 1944 a European Advisory Commission, composed of representatives appointed by Britain, Soviet Russia and the United States, decided on the partition of Germany into zones, the details being worked out according to an earlier decision reached at the Moscow Conference of October 1943. Regarding Berlin, the agreement read: 'The area of Greater Berlin will be occupied by troops of each of the Four Powers. An inter-allied governing authority, consisting of four commanding officers appointed by their respective Supreme Commanders, will be established to administer it jointly.'

In the dramatic last hours of Hitler's life, as the Soviet armies surrounded the city, overcoming fierce resistance in house-to-house fighting, and finally capturing the Führer's bunker which had been built between the Brandenburger Tor and the Potsdamer Platz, the armies of the Western Allies remained at the River Elbe, leaving the Soviets a free hand in Berlin. Not till about two months later did the first contingent of an American military force arrive in the city.

Shortly after capturing Berlin, the Russians set up a Soviet Military Administration as the ruling authority for the whole of Berlin and for the Soviet-occupied zone of Germany. Simultaneously their Supreme Commander, Marshal Zhukov, issued an order dated 13th June 1945, which allowed the Germans to form political parties and 'free' trade unions provided these were all anti-fascist. This move came as a great surprise to the other Allies, who had neither been consulted nor even informed about it. However, at the Potsdam Conference on the 2nd of August, an order was issued allowing democratic parties to be formed everywhere in Germany, and this was put into effect in the American, British and French zones in the following months.

Meantime the leading officials of the German Communist Party, who had earlier fled to the Soviet Union, now returned—William Pieck and Walter Ulbricht among them—with the victorious Russian troops. With its leadership intact and the actual set-up of its organisation completed in advance, the Communist Party was in a position to take immediate action to win control, backed as it was by unlimited military power. Before the Western Allies reached Berlin, therefore, Communists were already heads of the Personnel and Administration Department, the Education Department, and the Labour and Social Affairs Department of the City administration. The organisation of the police force was wholly in their hands. Communists headed both the Traffic and the Criminal Departments. In like manner they tried to win control of the twenty boroughs into which the administration of Greater Berlin is divided, though without quite the same success. At any rate, by the time the

Western Allies arrived, the Communists had already laid a firm foundation for taking over Berlin.

With the arrival of American, British and French troops, Greater Berlin was now partitioned into four sectors, the Russians retaining eight of the boroughs in their sector, six going to the American sector, four to the British and two to the French. In a provisional constitution promulgated by the Occupying Powers, the decrees and directives of the City Government were defined as applying to the whole district of Greater Berlin (thus tacitly sanctioning the existing, largely Communist, set-up). Another section of this constitution stated that 'changes in the constitution, the resignation of the City Government or of any of its members, as well as the appointing or dismissing of leading officials in the City administration, can be carried out only with the approval of the Allied Kommandatura in Berlin.' In other words, the Soviet members of the Kommandatura could veto any changes not to their liking. The Communists already placed in key positions in the City Government and its administration were thus well protected.[1]

It was not possible, of course, entirely to prevent non-Communist political parties from beginning to organise, but there were many ways in which influence could be brought to bear in such a situation. Food was very short. With the co-operation of Communists in the administration, Communists in the newly formed 'Free German Trade Union Federation' were made responsible for the distribution of potatoes, rhubarb and various

[1]Similar moves were made to control the trade unions. A 'Free German Trade Union Federation' was launched with an executive composed of three Communists, three Socialists and two Christians or Liberals, all from unions which had been in existence prior to the time when Hitler closed them down. The Communists then succeeded in persuading the Socialists to accept an Otto Brass, just back from Moscow, as one of the three Socialist representatives. He turned out to be a trained Communist. Shortly after, the two remaining Socialist representatives went over to the Communists. Of sixteen trade unions, the leadership of fourteen was entirely in the hands of the Communists. Ninety per cent of the works-committee members in all industries in Berlin were Communists. The headquarters of this trade-union movement was located in the Soviet sector.

other foods. In the hunger-ridden first months after the end of the war, those who controlled such food supplies were very popular. Then there was the question of office space in a city where so much stood in ruins. A few days before the Western Allies were due to arrive in Berlin, the Socialists were persuaded to move from their small and rather inadequate headquarters in the Zietenstrasse, in what was to become the American sector, to the spacious former Dresdner Bank made available for them in the Soviet sector. Similarly the Christian Democrat's headquarters was moved from what was to become the British sector over to the Soviet sector.

Meanwhile in different parts of Berlin, small groups of Social Democrats had been meeting together. Representatives from these different groups formed a central committee which they designated the Socialist Party of Germany, the SPD. Their programme was—'Democracy in state and municipality, Socialism in economic affairs and in society.' One of their leading men was a former member of the Reichstag, Otto Grotewohl. Through a mixture of promises and pressure, he and his friends were got into negotiations with the Communists for a 'united front' between the two parties. After some time the outcome was the calling of a conference of all the Berlin SPD officials to bless their central committee's decision to fuse with the Communist Party, the KPD, and form a new 'Socialist Unity Party of Germany', the SED.

The conference was fixed for the 1st of March 1946, at the Admiralpalass in the Soviet sector. In the courtyard and in the street outside the Admiralpalass Russian soldiers were drawn up. Lines of other Soviet soldiers with fixed bayonets stood on guard in the corridors and in the hall where the meeting was to be held. Otto Grotewohl made a two-and-a-half hour speech explaining the decision of the central committee to amalgamate with the Communists in the new SED Party, and declared himself in favour of this move.

Anyone opposing had only his own deep conviction to go on.

In the circumstances, there was not even any guarantee of his personal safety. However, Franz Neumann, a metal worker from the Reineckendorf Borough in the French sector, rose and opposed the decision. In a vigorous, fighting speech he argued that a decision to fuse the two parties could only be properly taken by an All-German Party conference of the SPD. 'A uniting of parties is not a thing that can be ordered,' he said. 'It can only be decided by the members themselves.' He put forward the suggestion that instead of sanctioning the central committee's decision, a referendum should be held. The audience was electrified. Neumann's motion was carried on the spot by an overwhelming majority. The delegates had demanded a referendum.

Permission for the referendum was granted by the Four Power administration of Greater Berlin and about a month later the referendum was held. In the Western sectors, where about 25,000 members voted, 82·5 per cent voted against the fusion of the two parties, while only 12·3 per cent voted for it. In the Soviet sector, when the workers went to the polling stations on the 31st March 1946, they were stopped by Russian officers and turned away. In total disregard of the referendum, Grotewohl and his committee went ahead anyway and obediently amalgamated with the Communist Party (KPD) thus forming the 'Socialist Unity Party' (SED). They then announced that the Socialist Party (SPD) had ceased to exist. My friend Georg told this part with certain grim relish. 'There you have the People's Democracy,' he said. 'A minority who have 82·5 per cent of the members against them decide that the majority no longer exists!'

An extraordinary situation had now arisen. In the Soviet sector and indeed throughout the Soviet zone of Germany, the SPD and the KPD had both been merged into the SED. But in the British, French and American sectors of Berlin, and throughout their zones of Germany, the SPD and the KPD existed side by side, leaving the SED unrecognised. Since, however, by Four Power agreement, no political party could be formed on a sector basis and since no party had any standing without the Four Powers' authorisation, neither the SED nor the SPD had any recognised legal status in Berlin itself.

The Socialists in the three Western sectors who had broken with the Grotewohl-led central committee now formed their own SPD executive and elected Franz Neumann as president. In order to be acknowledged they then had to apply to the Four Power Kommandatura for a licence. This faced the Kommandatura with a delicate situation. If the Soviet vetoed the application of the SPD (now banned in their sector), the Western Allies might veto the SED application. After prolonged discussions it was agreed to compromise and license both, and this was done on the 31st of May.

With the licensing of the political parties, the ground was now prepared for an election, and this was soon demanded. The Soviet commandant turned down the request. At the insistence of the other three commandants, however, the request was sent on to the highest Allied authorities, who finally agreed to authorise an election and the date of the 20th of October was fixed.

A real election campaign started—the first in Berlin since Hitler had come to power in 1933. The results made world news. Out of the 130 seats in the City Parliament, the SPD won sixty-three, the SED only twenty-six. The CDU (Christian Democratic Party) was second with twenty-nine seats and the LDP (Liberals) won twelve.

Theoretically the non-Communist parties were now in power. But it soon turned out that a No vote in the City Parliament by the SED was backed up by a Soviet veto in the Kommandatura. This is where the paragraph, 'changes in the constitution, the resignation of the City Government or any of its members, as well as the appointing or dismission of leading officials in the City administration, can be carried out only with the approval of the Allied Kommandatura in Berlin' (see page 138), came in. Thus two candidates for ministerial posts who had the support of the overwhelming majority of the City Parliament had to be replaced by others acceptable to the SED and the Soviet members of the Kommandatura. In the eight boroughs of the Soviet sector the results of the elections were virtually cancelled out by a decree from the Soviet sector Kommandatura ordering that no changes of personnel whatever in the borough administration could be made without their approval. Incidentally the City Parliament building itself was in the Soviet sector.

This was a life-and-death struggle, as more and more people began to realise. The conflict came to a head when the Berlin City Parliament, by a vote of eighty-five to twenty, passed a motion censuring the then Lord Mayor and demanding his resignation. For some weeks the struggle grew more and more intense. The SED at last realised they could not hope to win by parliamentary methods. On the 23rd June 1948, the Communists stormed the City Parliament building in the Parochialstrasse and so brought about the final division of Berlin. The non-Communists parties moved the government into the Schöneberg City Hall in the American sector.

The next day, 24 June, the Soviet Military Administration announced that all railway transport between Berlin and the West had been stopped. On the pretext that the bridge across the Elbe at Magdeburg was under repair, road transport on the autobahn had also been stopped. The three Western sectors of Berlin were cut off. West Berlin had become virtually a besieged city overnight.

It was then that the American Commander, General Clay, along with the British and the French, created the airlift, one of the greatest technical and operational feats the twentieth century had seen. Every third minute, night and day, in sun or rain or fog or storm, a plane touched down in West Berlin. They brought food, coal, clothing, oil, machinery—everything the beleaguered city needed. The high point in the delivery of these airlift cargoes was 13,000 tons in one day. In the spring of 1949 airlift imports were averaging 8,000 tons a day, an amount equal to what was daily being brought in by rail and canal before the blockade began.

The Berliners like to recall those days, Georg said. There was need, tension, many difficulties to be faced, but they felt the battle was worthwhile. At one point the Soviet authorities cut off the electrical supply. West Berlin was suddenly without light, without power. But heavy machinery and construction materials for the building of a big power station at Spandau in the British sector were brought in by the airlift and put together at high speed, making West Berlin independent of the Soviet sector for electricity. So the Berliners, who had heard the roar of the bombers overhead in wartime, were heartened and encouraged by the roar of these airlift planes. To them it sounded like a symphony of freedom and solidarity with the free world.

On 12th May 1949, a little more than eleven months after it had begun, the blockade was lifted. West Berlin was still free.

II

In Berlin the 1st of May is a very special occasion. Not only the workers, but the whole population rallies for a demonstration. Some of us were in the city in 1952 and the 1st of May Committee invited us to be their guests at the rally. In addition to trade-union leaders from many parts of Europe, the West German President, Dr. Heuss, and the Lord Mayor of Berlin, Ernst Reuter, were to address the crowds. We saw people in their thousands converging on the huge open Platz der Republic, one side of which, beyond the burnt-out shell of the Reichstag, borders on the Soviet sector. There were workers from Siemens, from the A.E.G., from Borsig, and other well-known firms. There was a great block of the transport workers, another of the building trades, and so on, endlessly. Some carried placards and banners, but these were comparatively few. What struck us most was the quietness of it all—no singing, no shouting. They just came from every direction in their tens of thousands, streaming through the wilderness that had once been the proud, royal Tiergarten park, or marching down the North-South Axis road, that wide and spacious thoroughfare where the SS used to parade, past the spot where Hitler formerly stood to take the salute and receive the adulation of the masses as his followers marched past. But all that is now a mass of rubble and desolation.

When we were shown to our seats on the platform, we looked out over a vast sea of faces. More than half a million people were there that day, according to the newspapers. These were the Berliners, people who had already endured more than most, people who could not easily be fooled. One felt their will to hold out, their determination to exist in freedom, their longing for an answer. Lord Mayor Reuter described the huge gathering as a 'proud confession of faith in the fight for freedom and of solidarity with the western world', and called for more help in the reconstruction and rebuilding of the city. He also stressed the point that the free world should steadfastly maintain its right of access to Berlin.

That May Day served to underline the problem. To the right of the Reichstag ruins we could see the tall columns of the Brandenburger Tor and the Red Flag flying over it. A mile beyond, another May Day demonstration was going on, only there everything was organised—the armed 'People's' Police, the Communist youth organisations, girls as well as boys also carrying guns, the orderly marching rows of workers, all in the style of the May Day parade outside the Kremlin in Moscow.

Division is the ever-present reality. Geographically, politically, economically, socially, Berlin, like Germany itself, is split in two. Even families are divided. A Berliner can stand in one of the Western sectors and look across the dividing line at his own house where he may no longer live—in freedom. The stark reality of the situation stirred me deeply. I felt it physically. Wherever I went, whoever I met, whatever I read I came up against it. Here the ideological struggle was even more acute than in the Ruhr. For it is the meeting place of two worlds—the western world with all its glamorous materialism, and the Communist world with all its ruthless materialism. It makes Berlin no easy place to live in. Spying of all kinds, smuggling, vice, shadowing and kidnapping, go on continuously. While I was there, people were shocked when a well-known lawyer in West Berlin, a leading figure in an organisation investigating and making public reports of crimes against humanity taking place in the Soviet-occupied zone, was knocked down one morning in broad daylight, dragged into a car and driven off at top speed across the sector border where the barriers were raised to let the car through and then dropped behind it to stop pursuit. It turned out later that his charming private secretary had been a Communist agent. She returned to East Berlin after the job was done and testified against the lawyer.

Then there was the constant flood of propaganda over the Soviet-controlled German radio stations. In the middle of a good musical programme the music would fade out and the voice of a professor, or a housewife, or a mechanic, in passionate accents, would urge western listeners to oust the Adenauer government and get rid of the 'warmongering lackeys of American imperialism' and so forth. It may sound funny but it can wear people down in the long run. The Berliners know perfectly well that, from a purely military point of view, their city could be taken in a matter of hours. Yet their determination to live in freedom remains unshaken. They see the challenge is a moral challenge, and to that they respond. As my friend, Georg, said: 'The moment Berlin shows moral weakness, or any disunity creeps in among us, the battle is lost. We have to live and act courageously. When politics and moral standards are in harmony, then the free nations will lead the world. Then trust in free society and democracy will grow. That is where Berlin depends on you and on the spirit of Caux.'

III

It was during another of my visits to Berlin that the day of my father's seventy-fifth birthday drew near. I was filled with a longing to go home to Oslo for it. True, my parents wrote me frequently, whole-heartedly backing me up in the work I was doing, and I was continually encouraged by that. But a father's seventy-fifth birthday is a great occasion. I would have dearly loved to be home for it. However, it so happened that a conference and a training course for youth in Berlin coincided with the date. As part of this course Georg and other trade-union leaders and industrialists were coming to speak. When we talked it over it seemed rather impossible for me to return to Norway at that particular time. So I wrote home and explained the situation. I also sent a special 'Address' to my father, in which I attempted to express to him all that he had meant to me.

After the birthday, my mother and father wrote me in detail about it. Imagine my delight as I read their letter! On the day before the anniversary, mother had been baking in the kitchen. The phone rang. It was the German Consulate in Oslo. Could she receive the German Ambassador to Norway at her home the next day? Yes, she said, completely taken by surprise. Then she rang up my Grini professor and others of our friends, who all undertook to come along to help. Next day, at the appointed hour, a car drew up at our gate and out stepped the German Ambassador and his wife, carrying a large bouquet. First there were introductions. Then everyone sat down to coffee and cakes and smørbrød. By and by the Ambassador rose and made a speech of congratulations to my father, adding that he wanted to thank both father and mother for permitting their only son to come to his country and for the way their son and his friends had been tirelessly working for the moral reconstruction of Berlin and Germany. It was evidently a very warm speech and absolutely unexpected. My parents were deeply touched. The last Germans they had seen in their home had been the ones who arrested me. This represented for them a very different Germany.

In Berlin, as in the Ruhr, our fight was not a political struggle but the fight for men.

The conference that had coincided with my father's birthday

was one of many. The Berliners were always encouraged by our visits and by the knowledge that they were not forgotten but were as much a part of the free world as ourselves. From 1947 on, many people from Berlin had been able to come to Caux. The friends they had made there from many countries were ready to support them in every way. Irène Laure with a group visited Berlin during the days of the blockade via the airlift. Miners from the Ruhr came several times. With my own eyes I saw what it meant to the Berliners to have guests from abroad in their city—Government officials from Thailand, Socialist M.P.s from Japan, national leaders from all parts of Africa. It meant just as much to the visitors too and built bridges, through men, throughout the world.

In October 1952, fifteen of Berlin's leading citizens sent a request to Dr. Frank Buchman asking that a group along with the international chorus from Caux should visit Berlin. 'Berlin feels the effects of world disunity to a very special degree,' they wrote. 'It is open for a message which would bring unity, thereby affecting everyone—all nations, races, classes and faiths.' So every time we came, I can remember that the first eager questions always were—"When is the international chorus coming? when will you bring your plays to Berlin?"

In the spring of 1956 the musical play, 'The Vanishing Island', together with several other plays by Peter Howard, came to Germany. With the casts, this made a force of 296 people from all five continents. They had been invited to Germany by Chancellor Adenauer, Foreign Minister Dr. von Brentano, and a group of other public figures. 'At this time of confusion in Europe and especially in divided Germany,' read the invitation, 'we need an ideology that brings clarity and moral force into the shaping of international relations as well as our own national life.'

'The Vanishing Island' and the other plays were given in Bonn, in Düsseldorf and all the major cities of the Ruhr, in Hanover. On 9th February the whole force flew into Berlin.

It was a long-awaited and much discussed event. The reports and pictures in the Berlin press showed a measure of the City's response. Under the headline, 'They have withstood the baptism of fire in Berlin', the 'Kurier' wrote:

'For the MRA mission to come to Berlin was probably the boldest move in their tour of the capitals of the free world. Only genuine commitment in every single one of them could ensure the response from Berlin hearts. The performances of "The Vanishing Island" and the play, "We are Tomorrow", showed that the real commitment of the actors met an equally honest response, so that actors and audience became a harmony.'

Every time the plays were presented, it was an experience to watch the crowds in the huge Titania Palast theatre. It gripped me to see how eagerly and intently they followed every word. They absolutely drank it in. The many in the audience who had bought the full printed text of the play (in German) followed it closely, line by line, all the pages turning together with an audible rustle. During 'The Vanishing Island' you could see the heads nodding when it came to the lines:

> 'No need to fear an alien creed of hate
> Even when it's knocking at the very gate—
> Provided we've a faith that hate to out-fashion,
> And live and give it with an equal passion.'

At a reception in the spacious Brandenburger Hall of the Schöneberg Rathaus, the Deputy Mayor summed it up. 'Your visit has already had the widest repercussions in Berlin,' he said. 'Many thousands have been shaken who said they would never be shaken by MRA. An aim to reshape the destiny of the world,' Mr. Amrehn continued, 'can only succeed if we control the forces in governments and nations. You have not been without success in getting governments and nations to take a new road and a new way of thinking. A minority—an influential minority —can change the destiny of nations. In our City of Berlin we are not only in the midst of a material struggle but find ourselves also in a spiritual struggle which challenges us personally every day. In such a situation we are grateful that you have come.' Willy Brandt, who at that time was President of the City Parliament, described the coming of this ideological mission as a 'great inspiration to our City'. Now Lord Mayor, he later added: 'The moral values of which you have spoken and which should be decisive in the relations between individuals, must also be accepted by the nations and the races. What I would like to see is not just normal relations between nations. We need more—a world community built on these moral standards.'

Radio Free Berlin, in a broadcast beamed for both East and West Germany, followed the evening news bulletin on the 1st March with a talk entitled 'A Renaissance that unites East and West' by Peter Howard:

'Berlin holds the attention of the world today. Berlin can give the world the answer. A renaissance of the human spirit could come to pass so simply and in such a way that the world would say, "That is the way all men are meant to live". Such revolution, such renaissance would powerfully impact the policies of Washington and of Moscow. It would affect human history. That is the hope and faith the world focuses on the citizens of Berlin.'

A letter from my friend Peter Petersen (see p. 55) clearly shows the response from the East as well as from the West. He had been in Berlin during the showings of the African film 'Freedom' at the time of the 7th International Film Festival in the summer of the following year.

'Dear Leif', he wrote, 'Berlin is at its very best these days. In spite of the heat wave over most of Europe, the invigorating air of Berlin seems to make her more alive than any other place.

'Yesterday, besides all the Festival showings and one for the Free University, the Africans had the opportunity of showing their film to an audience from the East. News that 'Freedom' was an MRA film brought 2000 people crowding into a cinema about a hundred yards from the sector border. My wife Ilse and I stood at the door watching the crowds coming in. Their faces seemed grey, their eyes tired, their clothes much more shabby than ours in West Germany. A young Englishman was standing by the door with a camera round his neck. My wife suddenly noticed that everybody seemed to be shying away from his neighbourhood—they knew what it would mean if their picture should by any chance be sent to the authorities! So we asked him to put his camera away.

'There was very little reaction from the audience during the first hour or so of the film. It was as if these people had long since stopped reacting spontaneously to anything. Then, towards the end, when the real ideological battle emerges clearly on the screen and they saw a positive answer being presented, the atmosphere suddenly changed. It was like something electric. You could hear people whispering, repeating some of the key sentences. You could feel the excitement growing and the applause at the close of the film was like an explosion. People came running down the centre aisle to meet us, shouting and applauding, tears running down their faces.

'We could hardly get away, so many wanted to speak to us. A man came up and said, "You will never know how much it means to us to see that there is a new ideological force at work in the free world. It is like being given a new lease of life." A family surrounded us and told how they had come all the way from Leipzig where a rumour about "Freedom" had reached them. They had stayed for a few days in the Soviet sector (of Berlin), checking every day with the cinema until they found out the right date and time.

'We spent another two hours with about 60 young men and women who just would not let us go. I have very rarely been through such a lively discussion, and you know how we Germans love discussions. But I have never heard so many questions which were so much to the point. Near the end of the two hours a young fellow of about our own age jumped up and said, "I have seen your film and I have heard you explain what this life and this ideology mean. I am convinced. But how can you dare to expect us to live this ideology in a police state?" One of his friends got up and said very quietly, "You know I am a Christian, but tonight I have seen how often I have excused my compromises by pointing to the dangers of living a Christian life in our state. From what I have experienced here I have come to two conclusions. The first is that no policeman can stop me from listening to God. The second is that God knows our situation even better than the secret police." The young fellow nodded.

'They all went back to the East. As you know, we cannot be in touch with them directly but something has been started in the hearts of these people which cannot be stopped. I keep wondering, Leif, whether these people who have lived under Hitlerism, and for the last 13 years under Communism, are not prepared by God to bring a challenge and an answer to us in the West. Only God knows how that can come about. But since last night I have a very real hope that one day it will be so. Whenever I get tired or discouraged I will remember those eyes and the hope that was in them as they left the cinema. You could see the difference in the faces as they arrived and in the faces as they left four hours later.'

IV

In all my experiences in Berlin perhaps the most vivid and memorable days were in the summer of 1956 when a large group of us were invited there, this time with two of the plays, 'We are Tomorrow' and 'The Dictator's Slippers', in German. Like all the other visits this one, too, had been made possible financially by people digging deep into their own pockets and by the sacrifices of thousands of men and women in West Germany and in other countries. The Berliners understood and responded to that kind of commitment and sacrifice where no one was paid, but instead everyone contributed freely their earnings and savings and all they had to these 'vital ideological missions', as the Berliners called them.

With the German cast there were in this group several Scandinavians, including the Finnish landowner (see page 99) and, among the Norwegians, Conrad Lauritzen, a business man of sixty-nine, who had been, for many years, director of a textile mill in Oslo. We had seen quite a lot of one another the previous summer in Caux, when he had been finding it very difficult to be free from his feelings against Germany. What he felt was very understandable when I heard his story.

He and his wife had lost their eldest son, also named Conrad, in the war. They had put much hope and trust in him, but when he had gone to Germany he had been strongly attracted by the idealistic side of National Socialism, and in 1942 had joined the German army only to be killed in action. To the Lauritzens it seemed as if Germany had robbed them of their dearest possession and the loss remained an open wound in their hearts. 'I cannot help feeling bitter against Germany', he told me.

That summer he was on the point of retiring from his job, and was planning to spend the remainder of his days quietly enjoying life in the country on his farm, a lovely spot overlooking the Oslo fjord, where he has often showed me around. His health was giving cause for concern, and country life would be just the thing.

In Caux, however, Conrad Lauritzen and his wife together took a revolutionary step. They decided to put all they had into the fight for men and the remaking of nations and to go whereever God wanted them to go. This brought a liberation from within which changed their entire attitude towards Germany. So now Conrad was in Berlin, speaking from the stage of the Titania Palast where 'The Dictator's Slippers' was being shown every evening. This was the same theatre where 'The Vanishing Island' had taken Berlin by storm a few months earlier, and now these plays in German were doing the same.

Many came from Potsdam, Magdeburg, Dresden, Leipzig, as

soon as the word got around that these plays were being given in Berlin.

Certain workers who had escaped from the East at the risk of their lives came to the plays evening after evening. Conrad met them and talked with them. 'We want to live this way,' they said. 'We are willing to risk our lives again for this idea that is the hope of the future. These amazing plays have brought a new factor to our notice, one that we have overlooked up to now. We have experienced a world of force and slavery. We have come into a world of comfort and indifference and apathy. But we see in MRA a world force which is bridging all divisions.'

A man who had just returned to West Germany, after eight years as a prisoner in Russia, saw 'The Dictator's Slippers'. He came up to one of the cast afterwards. 'I never dreamt that such an answer was at work in the world,' he said. 'I have read widely, talked to people, gone to innumerable plays, done everything to find in the West what I and my fellow prisoners have longed for. Tonight is the first time since my return from prison that I have found any hope.'

For the crowds that could not get into the theatre, meetings were held near by. Conrad Lauritzen had been one of the speakers each evening. On the 5th June he had just spoken from the stage in the Titania Palast before the curtain went up and was on his way up the stairs to the parallel meeting in the City Hall, when he had a sudden heart attack and died. He was quite well aware that this might be his last journey. Before leaving Oslo friends had warned him that it would be unwise to go to Berlin. But Conrad had replied, 'Humanly speaking you may be right. But I feel it is right to go. Out of hate and bitterness no peace can come and we who have been given an answer must take the lead in forgiving.' Over and over again he had said, 'We are all responsible, together with the Germans, for creating a new spirit in Europe.'

The following night in the Titania Palast Peter Petersen stepped out in front of the curtain before the performance. He told the audience of Conrad's death. Then he opened the notebook Conrad had left behind. 'These are the last words Conrad Lauritzen addressed to us Germans,' said Peter, and went on to read what Conrad had given from the stage the previous evening:

'I fought against Germany as an officer in the Norwegian Resistance and my youngest son fought with me. My eldest son, who studied in Dresden, was won by the National Socialist ideology, volunteered for the German Army, and lost his life in Russia in a German uniform. I have found liberation from bitterness through a change of heart. That is why I have come here and why I want to give my life that Germany finds her true destiny.'

Spontaneously the whole audience of nearly 2,000 rose to its feet and stood in silence.

Conrad Lauritzen's body was brought home by air to Oslo on the 7th June. Just before the plane arrived his wife received a message he had sent to her from Berlin on the day of his passing. 'I feel very much at home here fighting with this force,' he had written, and he ended, 'I hope to be home on the 7th.'

Two days later the Oslo daily, 'Vart Land', said of him: 'He was unshakeable in his decision to give everything in the fight for this idea he had dedicated his life to. . . . . He was not only a warm-hearted person. He was also a statesman of the type the world needs today.'

14
Road to Europe

ONE of my friends is a well-known journalist. His books have been read by millions. On occasions he met an ambassador who for many years had served his country in Communist Russia. The ambassador was one of the very few who became an intimate friend of Josef Stalin. At a dinner they had together shortly before the end of the Second World War, Stalin made a fierce attack on Germany.

'Why do you do that?' the ambassador asked.

'You do not understand ideology,' Stalin answered. 'The greatest danger to Communism is a united Germany. We are never going to let Germany rise united again.'

The leaders of the Kremlin have always known that the Soviets' man-power and resources, coupled with the industrial potential of Germany, would constitute the strongest power in the world.

These have been the motives behind all Communist strategy in regard to post-war Germany. It became evident in the struggle to win control of the coalmines and the steel factories of the Ruhr (1947–50), and equally evident in Berlin at the time of the blockade and the air lift. While Stalin used threats and terror to achieve his goals, his successors turned to smiles and talk of co-existence, but the activities of the Kremlin remained the same: separating West Germany from the rest of the world and infiltrating Ruhr industry with agents to prepare for the day of take-over. Again in 1959, Berlin was in the headlines all over the world. An ultimatum from Moscow threatened a new blockade or worse if the Western Powers refused to abandon the two and a half million free Berliners to be swallowed up by the Communist-dominated

East Berlin régime. Again, however, the West stood firm and the threat was averted, at least for the time being.

The two men who, more than any others, represent this determination to avert Communist take-over are Chancellor Dr. Adenauer and West Berlin's Lord Mayor Willy Brandt. Although of opposing political parties, they are both clear-sighted statesmen who know from experience that on the ideological level there can be no such thing as co-existence. They know that the men in the Kremlin are out to win the world. They feel that if Berlin is lost, West Germany will be lost; if West Germany is lost, Europe will go and America may in the end be forced to capitulate. They are both determined that the free world shall understand the global strategy of Communism.

It should surprise no one, therefore, that both men have been the objects of constant and deliberate Communist attack; obviously the Communists, in their effort to divide the West, try to play on the old fears of Britain and France by painting the ghost of German militarism and Neo-Nazism on the walls.

Is there anything the ordinary man can do about world events? Some of the Ruhr miners thought there was, and it was from the Nordstern Pit in Gelsenkirchen that the answer began to emerge.

One of the miners there, Hans Hartung, a member of the works committee, went with his wife to the Summit Strategy Conference in Caux in the summer of 1959. A passionate young Socialist, Hartung lived in the social and political struggle for his country. Deeply concerned about the Communist infiltration from East Germany and systematic subversion of Ruhr and German industry, and alert to the changing moods of the world situation, he realised that unless we reconstruct democracy from within there will be no future. The real danger, he told me, was not Communism but the decadence of the free world. He decided that nothing would stop him from bringing the answer to the world. He made simple moral decisions in his own life and became a free man.

The ideology of Moral Re-Armament was to come first in his life from now on. He at once told his wife, Irmgard, a hard-working mother of four children. They live vividly in my imagination from the many days we spent together in their flat just a short distance from the coalmine. Irmgard was usually in the kitchen washing and ironing, or with us in the living-room sitting at the sewing-machine, making new clothes for the children. But she always had time to give us a cup of good German coffee. Hans and I would sit and discuss a book he was writing, while their two youngsters, Hans Jorgen and Klaus Dieter, would come storming in, black as soot after their explorations in the streets and playgrounds. Irmgard would clean them up and say to her husband, 'You are no intellectual, Hans, you cannot write a book.' And often when she found his writings floating around they would go into the waste-paper basket. This was a sore point in the family.

When Hans told her in Caux about his new decision, she also committed herself to the same fight. And she decided not to try to control his life any more or nag him about his writing, but to back him one hundred per cent in his conviction.

Early next morning Hans was teeming with ideas, and by the end of the evening he had conceived a play with the answer to the challenge to Communism and to the indifference of the free West. He called it 'Hoffnung'—'Hope'. In two days it was tried out on the stage in Caux—with triumphant success.

Back in the Ruhr their colleagues in the Nordstern mine and their miner friends such as Kurowski, the Bladecks, the Wegerhofs and Heskes—a force of fifty altogether—met for a reading of the play. The miners' families responded and soon they had a cast. Every evening, after a hard day's work, they met for rehearsals. One day the thought came to them, 'Take "Hope" to Berlin'.

At first it looked impossible. The miners had to get leave from their different pits. It was difficult at that time in the Ruhr coal-mining industry. Millions of tons of coal were piled up unused.

Pits were being closed. The future looked very insecure, especially for those miners who were not right on the spot. The wives who went with them would have to make arrangements for their homes and children. There was the question of money. And many other points.

But they were clear it had to be done, and let no difficulties stand in the way. A few weeks later they were on the stage in the striking modern Kongresshalle theatre, which stands in the heart of Berlin's famous Tiergarten within sight of the ruined Reichstag Building and of the Brandenburg Gate where the Soviet and East German flags flutter in the wind.

Among the thousands who tried to get seats night after night were hundreds from the East Zone who streamed across the Sector border. They risked imprisonment in order to see 'Hoffnung'. So many came that the play had to be transferred to the huge 2,000-seat Titania Palast theatre. This was also crowded out. There was a tremendous response both to the play and to such speakers as Dr. Heinrich Vockel, representative of Chancellor Adenauer and Plenipotentiary of the Federal Government in Berlin. He expressed Berlin's thanks to the Ruhr miners and declared, 'If this force wins through to victory, we can have hope in future for a united Germany and for the liberty and peace of the whole world.' Similar response was given by the vast crowds to Robert Wegerhof. There were gasps in the theatre as he explained how he had been trained in Communism in Russia for five years, concluding, 'An ideological strategy to divide Europe must be answered by an ideological strategy to unite Europe. That is why we are giving "Hope" which is a weapon in that answering strategy. It shows how each one can have a part. Then we will win.'

Hope was echoed not once but many times by people from the East Zone who stayed on in the theatre to talk with the Ruhr miners and the cast. 'Do not be too concerned or fascinated by what goes on behind the Iron Curtain,' they would say. 'This ideology you have given through "Hoffnung" tonight is what is needed and you must concentrate on giving it to the millions in the free world while there is time. That is our best hope of one day being free too, the one hope of uniting our divided country, the one hope for all mankind.'

The people of Berlin have a clarity born of all they have been through, from which we could learn much. 'There are certain people in the West,' said Berlin's best known Churchman, Bishop Dibelius, most of whose diocese lies in the Soviet Zone, 'who seem to believe that Communism is just a different form of social order. These people have no inside knowledge of Communism. If Communism came to the West, Christianity would be submitted to a process of extermination supported by an authoritarian State machinery complete with a ruthless secret police. Yet there are even some who talk about the possibility of co-existence. Co-existence is like letting a tiger in with a sheep. Soon you need a new sheep.'

In Berlin the Ruhr miners received an invitation to bring 'Hoffnung' to Britain, signed by Members of Parliament of both parties, by members of the British Armed Forces, and by leading men in the Press, industry, and the trade unions. The cast decided to accept.

On the way from Berlin to Britain they stopped in Bonn, the West German capital, to give several further performances of 'Hoffnung' under the direct sponsorship of Chancellor Adenauer.

While the Chancellor was taking part in an important debate in the Bonn Parliament, he noticed the miners in their traditional uniforms in the gallery. He sent up a message to them to come for coffee with him in the room next to the plenary hall. There they talked together intimately for a full hour about their forthcoming visit to Britain.

London's *Sunday Times* reported this interview in a front-page story:

'Dr. Adenauer forecast that his forthcoming talks with Mr. Macmillan in London would end in "full agreement", but he added a warning that relations between the British and German people were still "under a certain cloud". "You have to clear away the fog," he said to the miners. "I will speak to Macmillan," continued the Chancellor, "you must speak to the British themselves. You will reach the masses. In you Britain will see the new Germany." And he added a sentence which Hans Hartung later repeated each night from the stage after the play—"We must never forget the wounds we have inflicted on other countries because we had a false ideology."'

A devout Catholic, Dr. Adenauer was an able administrator and was elected Lord Mayor of Cologne in 1917 at the early age of 41. So successfully did he steer the fortunes of the city during the difficult days of 1919 that in 1926 he was offered the Chancellorship of the German Reich, but he did not accept because of all the political parties' quarrels which would have made any stable government impossible. Seven years later Hitler came to power, but when he was going to make his first party speech in Cologne, Dr. Adenauer, as Lord Mayor, refused to meet him and ordered his city officials to remove the Swastika flags which Hitler's Storm Troops had placed on the Cologne bridge. A few days later the Nazis tried to assassinate Dr. Adenauer. But he got to know about it and escaped at the last moment.

After being removed from office, Dr. Adenauer spent a year in the sanctuary of the famous Monastery of Maria Laach. Then he left in order not to endanger the Monastery and was arrested by the Gestapo in 1934 and imprisoned at Potsdam. However, after interrogation, he was released and managed to stay in hiding till 1944, when twice in rapid succession he was re-arrested but miraculously managed to escape each time. With the coming of the Allied Armies he once more became Lord Mayor of Cologne, a city terribly destroyed and laid waste. On many points, however, he could not see eye to eye with the British military authorities and was relieved of his post.

He was now 69. Germany lay in ruins, both materially and

spiritually. Democracy would have to be built from the roots up. An answer would have to be created to Prussian militarism and to National Socialism. With the Russian armies Communism had made gigantic advances westward. Dr. Adenauer had long realised that only a new Germany and a united Europe could provide the answer, and in the ensuing years he devoted his life and energies to bringing this about. He has been like a great rock amid all the swirling, wishful, appeasing suggestions that nowadays go under the name of 'peaceful co-existence'.

From 1945 on, Dr. Adenauer saw the need for a united Christian front and was one of the main architects of the Christian Democratic Union, the party now in power in West Germany. In 1948 he became President of a Constituent Assembly formed by delegates from the different Land Parliaments of the American, British and French Zones, the body which preceded the formation of the Federal Parliament in Bonn. In 1949 Dr. Adenauer was elected as the first Chancellor under the new constitution. From the start he maintained—though this was not popular then—that Germany must earn her freedom little by little through a policy of co-operation with the Allies. He was opposed to German re-armament, except as a part of a European force. He strongly supported the Schuman Plan to put French and German coal and steel production under a common authority, a move which has led to the European Common Market. He sought friendship and reconciliation and understanding with France, though France and Germany had been hereditary enemies for a century or more. He sought to restore for the past to Israel and the Jewish people, and large reparations were voted by the Bonn Government. He took strong steps against any revival of totalitarian or racial ideas. As the British political writer and author, Peter Howard, said, 'All free men owe Dr. Adenauer an everlasting debt. Had it not been for his ideological clarity and steadfastness, Western European unity would have been shattered. He is the most clear thinking statesman in Europe.'

When the German Chancellor arrived in Britain on 17th

November 1959, for three days of official talks, his first appointment after being welcomed in London at Victoria Station by Mr. Macmillan was with his friends, the Ruhr miners, at the German Embassy. He listened intently to their report of 'Hoffnung' in the South Wales coalfields, the Rhondda and Cardiff, and of the scheduled performances in the dock area of East London, in the West End and in Scotland. He said to them, 'You are doing a great service to Britain and Germany, and to the cause of world peace.' When he heard that, after the visit to Britain, they had been invited to France, he added with emphasis—'Britain, France, Germany—that's it. That's right.'

That evening at a great public function given in honour of Dr. Adenauer by the Anglo-German Association, Mr. Macmillan said, 'Many of us spent the best years of our youth or middle age seeing our countries locked in bitter conflict. How splendid then it is to feel that we are now partners in the great enterprise of the preservation of peace and liberty throughout the world. We welcome you (Chancellor Adenauer) as the representative of all that gives us hope. You have done far more than the true patriotism of the European. You have looked beyond the confines of your country.'

When the Chancellor arrived at Victoria Station to take his leave, Mr. Macmillan pointed out the miners from 'Hoffnung', and the Chancellor bade them a warm farewell as the crowd broke spontaneously into singing 'For he's a jolly good fellow'.

In a broadcast to the nation after Dr. Adenauer's visit, Mr. Macmillan said, 'Britain and Germany must stand united. Chancellor Adenauer and I reached agreement on every point.'

What was it the Ruhr miners did?

They gave 'Hoffnung' in the mining town of Tonypandy in the heart of the Rhondda Valley. They gave it in Cardiff's Empire Theatre, in the Poplar Civic Theatre in East London and in the Saville Theatre in Shaftesbury Avenue. They gave it in Edinburgh and Glasgow. Their distinctive black traditional miners' dress and their tall plumed hats became familiar to millions on the television screen and through pictures in the Press. Thousands upon thousands crowded the theatres night after night to see the play and to meet the cast, and each night the audience was electrified to hear the German miners sing 'God save the Queen' before the play began.

The author describes it as a play which deals with the 'realities of the ideological struggle in the world today'. It is more than a play. It embodies the decisions of these Ruhr miners to tackle the most burning problems in Europe. It deals with the tyranny of the Communist régime in the East and the materialism and selfishness which leads to the false conception of freedom as practised in the West. It shows how delinquent youth, profit-blinded businessmen, ambitious trade unionists, ineffective clergy, and even Communist agents, find a world-uniting ideology based on absolute moral standards where God is in control and not man.

Certain events stand out in the scores of public engagements in which the miners took part during this visit to Britain.

There was Remembrance Sunday in Cardiff with the bands and detachments from the Army, Navy and Air Force, civil defence and ex-servicemen's organisations, the hushed crowd headed by Cardiff's Lord Mayor, then the Two Minutes' Silence, with the bugles sounding the Last Post. And there at the Welsh National War Memorial, amid all the other wreaths, the Ruhr miners, in their traditional dress, laid their simple wreath tied with the Federal German colours and inscribed 'From Miners of the Ruhr'. With their wives they joined in the hymns in their best English. After the parade they were invited to the British Legion headquarters to meet leaders of the Armed Forces and of the ex-servicemen's organisations.

In Edinburgh the Newton Grange Colliery Pipe Band, champion in many pipe-band contests, was waiting to welcome the Ruhr miners on the station platform. Pipes skirling and kilts swinging, the band marched in front of the miners out of the station and along Princes Street. At the end of the final performance in Glasgow a week later the same pipe band appeared on stage to the astonishment of both cast and audience, having come through specially from Edinburgh to give the Ruhr miners a real Scottish send-off. After the pipers had played 'Ye're no awa' tae bide awa'' the whole theatre spontaneously burst into 'Auld Lang Syne'. The Ruhr miners had certainly won the hearts of the Scots.

There was a civic reception in Glasgow's City Hall given by Lord Provost Sir Myer Galpern, M.P., a member of the Jewish faith. Speaking for all the Germans, Hans Hartung, much moved, told the Lord Provost—'I cannot ask you to forget the millions who died. But I do ask you to forgive and to help us build a future free from hate.'

'As a member of the Jewish faith, I am deeply touched,' replied the Lord Provost. 'We share your "Hope". I welcome you to the City of Glasgow and commend the work you have undertaken.'

'Britain, France, Germany—that's it. That's right,' Chancellor Adenauer had said.

From Britain 'Hoffnung' went to France. As in the Ruhr and the Rhondda, so in the coalfields of northern France, there was an overwhelming response to the drama from all who saw it.

Guy Mollet, Secretary-General of the French Socialist Party, former Prime Minister, Member of Parliament and also Mayor of Arras, headed the Committee of Invitation.

Enthusiastic was the response of the French audiences to 'Espoir' in Lens, Henin-Lietard, Puteaux and Paris itself, but even more moving were some of the visits the Ruhr miners made. When they were received by M. Mollet in Arras he expressed his concern that the idea of co-existence would lead to a dangerous softening up of the free democracies and that Khrushchev's coming visit to France would be used by the Soviets to split Western unity. The miners replied, 'We Socialists, who know that co-existence with Communism is not possible, should stand up and warn the world.' 'I fully agree,' said M. Mollet. 'It is my conviction that we will carry this fight through to victory.'

They visited the French National War Cemetery at Notre Dame de Lorette near Arras. There a towering monument stands sentinel amid the thousands of simple crosses marking the graves of 100,000 French soldiers who gave their lives in the fifteen-month-long battle that was fought over this mining area in World War I. Thousands of British and Canadian soldiers are buried on the nearby Vimy Ridge and neighbouring cemeteries.

At the steps of the monument the German miners and their wives and the representatives of seventeen nations with them sang the Marseillaise.

Then looking out over the crosses row on row, one of the German miners spoke, 'These graves have had to come about because our past has been filled with pride, hate and bitterness. They are a witness to the wrongs that have marked the relations between our nations in the past. We bow before the dead. We will fight shoulder to shoulder with the French people for the liberty, equality and fraternity of the world. Our commitment is to live and fight for Moral Re-Armament as this is the surest way to make certain that such loss and sorrow as these graves represent never come to pass again.'

After the miners had laid their wreath of roses, carnations and laurel in the shrine under the inscription, 'To the Unknown Heroes', the French priest in charge of Notre Dame de Lorette gave the MRA task force his blessing and added, 'The French and German soldiers—sons and fathers—who gave their lives, have tremendous joy that you are here together today. But God's joy is greater.'

In Paris 19th December 1959 was a significant day. That morning President Eisenhower, Chancellor Adenauer and Prime Minister Macmillan met at the Elysée Palace with General de Gaulle. The same morning General de Gaulle's niece, Madame

Anthonioz, well known in the French Resistance as Geneviève de Gaulle, received the Ruhr miners at the Mont Valerien Fortress, the national shrine of the Resistance movement. Here between 1940 and 1944, 4,500 hostages and Resistance fighters were shot by the Gestapo, who used the fortress as their Paris headquarters. It was the first time Germans had been received here since the war. Their visit was made on the advice of Chancellor Adenauer and to make public restitution for the losses caused by Nazism.

After laying a wreath, Hans Hartung, describing the stone of remembrance as marking 'one of the darkest places of our past', did, in the name of the Germans present, accept full responsibility for that past and said they 'solemnly pledged themselves to do everything that such tragedies do not happen again'.

Madame Anthonioz, a survivor of the Ravensbruck concentration camp and President of the French Women Deportees (to Germany) Association, replied, 'I would like very simply to thank you for coming. For us deportees it is a deeply moving occasion. I think I can say on behalf of myself and my colleagues that no hate or bitterness against your nation remains in our hearts. It is our earnest desire to give everything with you and with men of good will so that the spiritual values we were defending through our resistance shall be preserved forever.'

As she shook hands with the German miners she said, 'I think it is important that you understand what it was that so many of us in the Resistance fought for and died for. It was to defend the vital moral values that were being threatened by National Socialism. That is why you and we can stand united here today.'

When he visited General de Gaulle earlier in December, Chancellor Adenauer had said, 'We owe it to our own peoples to establish an irrevocable alliance between the French and German peoples and, with the free nations of our continent, lay the foundations of a united Europe. We intend to make our countries' future different from their past.'

That is what the Ruhr miners were doing. They were demonstrating in flesh and blood what they sang in the 'Song for Germany' at the close of their play—

> 'Through change of heart
> True unity comes.'

Unity in the West, Paul Kurowski once said, is more feared in the Kremlin than the atom bomb. The success of Chancellor Adenauer, supported by such actions as those of the Ruhr miners, in building ideological unity with the British and French people was so evident that the Kremlin reacted immediately.

The world Press was suddenly full of news that synagogues in every continent had been daubed with Swastikas by persons unknown. In whose interest could it be that the millions in Europe and America should tell themselves that Hitler's Nazism and anti-Semitism was here once again?

The leading French national daily, *Le Figaro*, put the finger on the spot in its editorial of 7th January 1960:

'What could have been considered at the outset as isolated incidents expanded into a perfectly orchestrated campaign. Orchestrated—but by whom? That is the question which is being asked in all capitals concerned. . . . The fact that such manifestations happen simultaneously in countries as different and as far apart as Finland and Australia leads one to conclude as the co-ordination is not in doubt, the words of evident command do not emanate from Federal Germany but from a centre better equipped for such a well-synchronised propaganda; and the mecca of Communism springs immediately to mind.

'Who but international Communism could be interested in sowing suspicions about West Germany on the eve of the East–West meeting, to make people believe in the renaissance of anti-Semitic Nazism in Germany and in the threat of its world ramifications? It is the best way to isolate Chancellor Adenauer and separate him from his allies. Besides, one has only to read the commentaries in the Soviet press to understand the meaning of this manoeuvre.'

Undeterred by the Kremlin's strategy to divide Germany from the rest of the free nations, 'Hoffnung' continued to move from strength to strength. In January 1960 requests came from leaders in India and from the Japanese Prime Minister for the play to visit Kerala and Japan, and from US Congressmen and Senators for it to go to Washington. Through the Chancellor's intervention, the men were released on pay by the German coal industry.

One of the leading newspapers of America, *New York Journal American*, published an exclusive article on Moral Re-Armament by Chancellor Adenauer which sums up the ideological battle in Europe and the world today:

'At this time of confusion in Europe we need, and especially in divided Germany, an ideology that brings clarity and moral power into shaping international relations. A nation with an ideology is always on the offensive. A nation without an ideology is self-satisfied and dead.

'Communism has gone through many phases—Marxism, Leninism, Stalinism, now Khrushchev. But one thing has remained unaltered—its aim of world domination. We must be prepared to continue the ideological struggle for several decades yet, but I am convinced Khrushchev's grandchildren will not be Communists.

'Dr. Frank Buchman, founder of Moral Re-Armament, is making a great contribution to international unity and to the establishment of social justice. A lasting memorial to his work is established in the hearts of mankind of this age. The way he has laboured to establish relationships between men and nations on firm foundations of moral values will never be forgotten.

'Now is the time to work more strongly than ever for European unity through MRA. A Europe in which freedom and brotherhood should reign can only be created when nations are mutually conscious of their moral responsibility. MRA has given most valuable stimulation to the great work of uniting Europe. Unless this work is carried forward, peace in the world cannot be maintained.

'Begin with yourself—that, in my opinion, is the basic challenge of MRA. May this challenge ring out far and wide across the whole world and into all nations.'

15
The Ideological Struggle

IT became clear to me during these years in Germany that Hitler's National Socialism and Leninist–Stalinist Communism have led to a tremendous shift in evaluating the worth of the individual. Man has become a means, a weapon in the ideological war. Going on around us there is a battle for our thinking, our feelings and our will, a battle whose outcome will lead whole continents either to freedom or to slavery. The twentieth century's total war for man—in industry, in politics, in the trade unions, in cultural life—is an ideological battle and no one can avoid living in its field of influence.

Foreign Minister Vishinsky put it this way, 'We shall conquer the world not with atom bombs but with our ideas, our brains and our doctrine.' Khrushchev, when Party Secretary, said at a gathering in Moscow, 'We are fully convinced that the Communist ideology will win everywhere in the world. We believe that and we are out for that.' Chancellor Adenauer has stated, 'We must be prepared to continue the ideological struggle for several decades.' Some years earlier President Eisenhower said, 'The battle that is going on in the world today is for men's minds and hearts. It is the ideological battle.'

What is the key to this drama in which, sooner or later, we must all play a part and in which, whether we like it or not, we are faced with a choice? That was the question I always came back to, driving home late at night through the factory towns of the Ruhr.

I shall never forget one evening in the late autumn of 1956 when we were in the home of Max Bladeck at Königsbergerstrasse 13, Moers, where he and his wife Grete had lived for the last twelve years. We were talking together in the kitchen, Max deep in an armchair beside the gleaming stove. Near him on the wall was hanging a violin. For Max was very musical. Besides the violin he could play the guitar, accordian and piano. He was unfit for work because of silicosis. The greater part of his stomach had already been removed and he weighed less than ninety pounds. But he was as tough as a terrier and a veritable force and energy emanated from him. He would listen carefully to the person he was with and when he himself spoke you had the feeling that Max not only understood but liked people.

That autumn evening the conversation had led to searching questions not only about ourselves but about the possibilities facing the Western world. Max brought up the subject of the last Party Congress in Moscow that Stalin had led. The dictator had expressed certain thoughts—basic Communist ideas which are just as relevant today, Max held—more or less as follows, 'The capitalist countries will destroy one another by their materialism and by competing against each other. We need only exploit their divisions—the tensions existing between races, classes, religions and nations. After a war between the capitalist countries we will be able to take over what is left. It will fall into our hands like ripe fruit.'

'This quadruple division between races, classes, religions and nations is one of the most important weapons in Communist world strategy,' Max underlined, 'and it is ruthlessly exploited all the time. Recently, when I visited most parts of the world with an international MRA team, we came across infiltration everywhere—in the films, radio, television and press, in the trade unions, in industry, in politics—an infiltration which exploits the weaknesses and moral defeats in men. Every one of the free nations in different ways is being ideologically undermined. It's not much help for a country to be armed militarily if it is split ideologically. If I, or my party, or my nation, create division in these four areas, then Communism will inevitably advance.

'The weakness of the West is that it lives materialistically. Our practice confirms what Communist theory proclaims. A Western world and a Communism which both build on materialism cannot develop anything new and worthwhile in man because their basic premise is untenable. Until they learn to solve the problems of human nature in a drastic and thorough-going way and on a national scale, nations must continue to take their historic road to violence and destruction. What the atomic age demands is new men.'

Max paused for a moment. He got up, went over to the table and took a notebook out of the drawer. He turned the pages—the neat writing looked almost like print. Passing a thin hand over his high forehead, he read:

'An ideology is the stream of faith and conviction constantly filling heart and mind and will with power for fresh action and effort.

'Today two ideologies face one another—one ideology with a firm belief in God, the other with a firm belief in no God.

'An ideology can be created by the intellect alone, as in the case of Hegel, Feuerbach, Marx and Lenin. Or it can be formed through inspiration from God. People who let themselves be led by an ideology are therefore either instruments for something man has created, an intellectual ideology that is not based on anything greater than man himself, or they are instruments in God's hands.

'Anyone who allows his own motives to be illumined and corrected by absolute moral standards and the guidance of God, will understand the ideological battle for people and will himself go into action. He will put right what is wrong in the world, starting with himself and his own nation.

'I have come to the conviction,' Max continued, 'that the deep roots of ideological confusion lie in moral compromise and defeat. When I break contact with the highest Truth, it is not God's fault but my own. That is why it is vitally important to take up the battle against hate and bitterness, jealousy and ambition, untruthfulness, impurity and selfishness which poison and blind man and bind him to themselves. Only when I am in fellowship with God do I fulfil my destiny.'

Such evenings with friends who had had years of experience in the Communist ideology helped me to a deeper understanding of the forces at work in our era and to see in wider framework and perspective all that I had experienced during the war years.

A few months after liberation in May 1945, I thought life was very difficult. Disillusionment had me in its grip. I recalled the clear, cold winter days in Grini when we walked along by the electric fence and looked out across the barbed wire to the open spaces beyond, drinking in the pure, clear air and longing for the day of liberation. But when freedom came things were not as I thought they would be. A heaviness came over me. What was really the point of living? One day, feeling like that, I said accusingly to my mother, 'Why did you bring me into the world? Wouldn't it have been much better if I had never been born?' Mother looked at me, her warm yet piercing eyes shining with understanding and love. 'Leif,' she said, 'there is so much evil in the world that we must bear children who will fight for the good.'

Her words remained with me and created a conviction which has become steadily stronger. Whether I will or not, I live in the midst of a battle between good and evil.

This tension is a part of life itself. 'The basic struggle,' as Frank Buchman says, 'is for the wills of men. That is the ideological struggle. It goes on in your heart and mine every day. The deciding factor is whether as men and nations we are guided by the voice of materialism or the Voice of God.'

In the eternal battle between good and evil there is no such thing as co-existence. I am in constant motion, inclining to the one side or the other, towards truth and liberation or towards lies and slavery, towards love and purity or towards hate and selfishness. Each new generation must take up the battle. For our generation today it is vital to make a clear choice. We are being bombarded with propaganda, lured by the shifting tactics of totalitarian dictatorship, promised everything in the name of false freedom. The chorus of confusing voices leads millions astray. What we need is clarity about the battle between good and evil, clarity on where we stand in that battle and what we do about it. Those engaged in this eternal struggle for man, committed to a moral ideology, will not be overcome by destructive forces either from within or from without, whatever guise these forces assume. Furthermore, they have the key to the second half of this century.

Was not the battle our German friends were going through in the Ruhr basically the same as the battle we in Norway had carried on during the occupation? Was not the choice Bladeck and Kurowski and the other revolutionaries had to make precisely the same choice that I and Hans had been faced with at Møller Street 19? The question was—were we to give in to human might, go against what we most deeply believed, and become slaves of a political system, or would we have the courage to choose what we knew was right: follow our conscience, and thus take the road of change and freedom?

In the past years I have met many men and women in leading positions, responsible people from all parts of the world. And I have got to know ordinary men and women. I have lived in their homes, shared the daily joys and sorrows of the family, especially their anxieties and worries about the future. I have seen how their thoughts and feelings centre around the possibilities of solving the vital but unsolved problems which the newspapers and politicians are concerned with. I have seen how solutions are proposed and then rejected one after the other.

Military arms? Necessary enough, but they cannot do more than provide a breathing space, a respite. Will not an anti-Communism that springs merely from fear and hate, in the long run poison us and make us slaves to the same evil forces that we are hoping to overcome?

To believe that 'peaceful co-existence' in itself will bring the answer, is to live in illusion. Leading Communists are very well aware that the idea of co-existence is no change of motive, but a mere change of tactics. It is just a means of lulling the free world to sleep while international Communism goes about re-shaping the world step by step in line with its plan, as undisturbed as possible. A democracy which does not know what it stands for will never be able to hold its position against a dictatorship with an aggressive ideology.

Everywhere people are wrestling with such problems today. But the thought has been borne in on me after many conversations late into the night that there is one question that goes much deeper.

There is a longing which is common to all mankind in both East and West, a longing for something great to live for, the faith through which both individuals and governments will commit themselves to truth, purity and right—the way of life which can set men free and unite them above the political systems that exist. There is something stronger than fear of atomic rockets and ideologies based on man. The strongest power in the atom age is God working in the heart of men. Those who possess such a liberating ideology will win.

When it comes to setting individuals free to live a life of destiny, Moral Re-Armament is the greatest thing I have met. It is the most audacious attempt to create a new civilisation.

There are only two ideologies bidding for the world. Communism and Moral Re-Armament. 'In one field we can make no compromise, and that is the ideological field. Ideological co-existence does not exist.' Khrushchev has said.

I believe that the ideology of Moral Re-Armament is the next step in human progress for the Communist and non-Communist world alike. It equips man in his everyday life with the answer to the dividing materialism which threatens mankind both from East and West. It is creating the new type of man—as much needed in Moscow and Peking as in London, Paris and Washington.

Man has to choose. What each one of us decides today will form the lives of generations for decades to come.

Here lies the opportunity for you and me, the millions, to lead humanity out of the evil situation with its two false alternatives, world Communist dictatorship or atomic war. It is Moral Re-Armament. Together we in East and West can fulfil man's destiny: to remake the world and usher in the greatest renaissance in history.

As I think of the future I am gripped by a deep sense of expectancy and wonder of the mystery I cannot understand, yet which I know from experience—that man, in spite of all his evil doing and his faults, is loved by God; that, through the cleansing power of Christ, we can rise from defeat and be lifted into a world of freedom and limitless possibilities; that everyone of us, wherever we are can receive this highest experience—the inspiration of God's Spirit to lead us throughout our lives.

This transforms the insecurity and hopelessness of the twentieth century into a great adventure.